T0323873

Why It's OK
to Be Amoral

Why It's OK to Be Amoral argues that self-righteous moralism has replaced religion as a source of embattled and gratuitous certainties. High-minded moral convictions invoke the authority of sacred moral truths, but there are no such truths. In reality, moral passions are rooted in atavistic emotional dispositions and arbitrary social conventions.

While public and private discourse is saturated with guilt, shame and righteous indignation, professional philosophers, under cover of clever argumentation, promote the utopian idea that all practical questions have uniquely right answers—providing that you adopt the right moral principles. But their justifications for those principles appeal to contested 'foundations', among which no rational adjudication is possible. Moreover, because there are two discrepant ways of understanding motivation, our access to agents' true reasons is never sufficiently reliable to warrant moral praise or blame. Finally, every agent has a wide diversity of reasons for action, yet moralists claim that some reasons trump all others, because they are 'moral' reasons. Since these too must be grounded in facts, that amounts to double counting some reasons.

Having exposed these aspects of the institution of morality, this book suggests that if we cannot abstain altogether from moralising, we can at least try to use it against itself.

Ronald de Sousa, Professor Emeritus of Philosophy at the University of Toronto, was born in Switzerland and educated at New College, Oxford (BA) and Princeton (PhD). He is the author of *The Rationality of Emotion* (1987), *Why Think? Evolution and the Rational Mind* (2007), *Emotional Truth* (2011) and *Love: A Very Short Introduction* (2015). A number of his interviews and debates are available on YouTube.

Why It's OK: The Ethics and Aesthetics of How We Live

ABOUT THE SERIES:

Philosophers often build cogent arguments for unpopular positions. Recent examples include cases against marriage and pregnancy, for treating animals as our equals, and dismissing some popular art as aesthetically inferior. What philosophers have done less often is to offer compelling arguments for widespread and established human behavior, like getting married, having children, eating animals, and going to the movies. But if one role for philosophy is to help us reflect on our lives and build sound justifications for our beliefs and actions, it seems odd that philosophers would neglect arguments for the lifestyles most people—including many philosophers—actually lead. Unfortunately, philosophers' inattention to normalcy has meant that the ways of life that define our modern societies have gone largely without defense, even as whole literatures have emerged to condemn them.

Why It's OK: The Ethics and Aesthetics of How We Live seeks to remedy that. It's a series of books that provides accessible, sound, and often new and creative arguments for widespread ethical and aesthetic values. Made up of short volumes that assume no previous knowledge of philosophy from the reader, the series recognizes that philosophy is just as important for understanding what we already believe as it is for criticizing the status quo. The series isn't meant to make us complacent about what we value; rather, it helps and challenges us to think more deeply about the values that give our daily lives meaning.

Titles in Series:

For further information about this series, please visit:
www.routledge.com/Why-Its-OK/book-series/WIOK

Why It's OK to Be Amoral

RONALD DE SOUSA

Why It's OK
to Be Amoral

Routledge
Taylor & Francis Group

NEW YORK AND LONDON

Designed cover image: Tara Moore/Getty Images

First published 2025
by Routledge
605 Third Avenue, New York, NY 10158

and by Routledge
4 Park Square, Milton Park, Abingdon, Oxon, OX14 4RN

Routledge is an imprint of the Taylor & Francis Group, an informa business

Library of Congress Cataloging-in-Publication Data
Names: De Sousa, Ronald, author.
Title: Why it's ok to be amoral : technologies of the self, government, and writing / Ronald de Sousa.
Description: New York, NY : Routledge, 2025. | Series: Why it's ok: the ethics and aesthetics of how we live | Includes bibliographical references and index.
Identifiers: LCCN 2024027335 (print) | LCCN 2024027336 (ebook) | ISBN 9781032235554 (hbk) | ISBN 9781032232836 (pbk) | ISBN 9781003278252 (ebk)
Subjects: LCSH: Self (Philosophy) | Self-righteousness. | Conduct of life. | Ethics.
Classification: LCC BJ324.S44 D47 2025 (print) | LCC BJ324.S44 (ebook) | DDC 170—dc23/eng/20240905
LC record available at https://lccn.loc.gov/2024027335
LC ebook record available at https://lccn.loc.gov/2024027336

ISBN: 978-1-032-23555-4 (hbk)
ISBN: 978-1-032-23283-6 (pbk)
ISBN: 978-1-003-27825-2 (ebk)

DOI: 10.4324/9781003278252

Typeset in Joanna and Din
by Apex CoVantage, LLC

Contents

A few preliminary remarks are called for about the terminology used in this book, its intended readership and the spirit in which it is written.

To begin with terminology. Of the three terms, 'morality', 'ethics' and 'metaethics', the first two are often equivalent, making the phrase 'moral and ethical'—like 'freedom and liberty'—little more than a pleonasm. Some wag noticed that 'ethics violations' are usually about money and 'immorality' is usually about sex. But when philosophers recognise a distinction, they are likely to think of morality as a set of rules, and of ethics as reflecting on much broader questions about how to live. In the latter sense, a concern with ethics is compatible with the rejection of morality that is amoralism (Marks, 2012).

As for 'metaethics', as the prefix 'meta' suggests, it is *about* ethics rather than part of it. It aims to explain what is distinctive about moral statements, oughts, values and principles.

Strictly speaking, while I am concerned to reject the need for and the authority of moral rules, much of what I have to say is about metaethics. But morality and metaethics have a way of seeping into one another's territory. Both Utilitarianism and Kantian Deontology, for example, belong strictly speaking to metaethics. But each has consequences for the moral question of what ought to be done or may be done in specific circumstances, and the precepts generated by different metaethical theories often conflict. So as to avoid getting lost in unnecessary quibbles, I will refer to 'moral systems' or 'moral theories' to denote systematic elaborations that in some cases might more precisely be classed as part of morality, while in others they would be better classed as pertaining to metaethics.

This book is a polemic. It is intended for readers who may wonder about what we mean when we talk about what morality commands or forbids, and what delimits the domain of moral as distinct from aesthetic, practical, personal or other domains of life we care about. My first contention is that among the general public a preoccupation with what is morally right or wrong, as opposed to all other reasons to care and to act, obscures rather than clarifies our judgments about what we have good reasons to do. My second claim is that the philosophers who have made a profession of justifying moral claims are doomed to keep thrashing in a morass of mutual question-begging. Among the rest of us, the supposed authority of morality encourages moralism, the self-righteous intrusion of guilt and blame, into every facet of our public and private lives.

By 'our', I mean to refer mainly to persons who, like me, live in a WEIRD (Western, educated, industrialised, rich and democratic) culture (Henrich, 2020). Although I shall sometimes refer to the diversity of existing cultures, and occasionally even to some non-WEIRD practices, that is the point of view from which I write, with all the limitations that implies.

To acknowledge those limitations, as well as those that derive from the accident of being an old, white, middle-class, European male, is to hint at the outset at my scepticism in regard to the prejudices and assumptions instilled into me, like anyone else, by the upbringing and life experience randomly allotted to each human being.

Although little I write in this book is original, I have been sparing in providing references, perhaps to the point of seeming ungrateful to the many writers who have said things I assert or discuss. Among those whose work has influenced me but to which I have not done justice, I must mention especially the authors of essays collected in the fine anthology edited by Richard Garner and Richard Joyce (Garner & Joyce, 2019), as well as to Joel Marks (Marks, 2012, 2016). Instead of listing all individual works to which I am indebted, I have wherever possible recommended entries from the *Stanford Encyclopedia of Philosophy*. The SEP presents several advantages: it maintains extremely high standards of professional competence, and endeavours to remain scrupulously up-to-date by requiring periodic revisions of all entries. It is freely available to anyone who can access the Internet. And every entry includes a cornucopia of citations and further readings. I have tagged SEP references by adding an asterisk to those citations.

A few friends and colleagues have very generously suffered through earlier drafts of this book in part or whole. In particular, I benefited from criticisms from Wayne Sumner, David Gallop, Robert D'Amico, Neera Badhwar and Christine Tappolet. I am especially indebted to Joel Marks, whose countless detailed and insightful comments on two successive drafts enabled me to make innumerable improvements in thought and diction, though not, I fear, to convince him that all his objections have been met.

I need to offer here a final note about the cover of this book. Those of you reading this in paperback or e-book form will no doubt notice on the front cover the image of a person balancing unsupported in mid-air. It was suggested by my imaginative and wonderfully supportive editor, Andrew Beck, to evoke a central tenet of this book: that reliance on an objective morality to guide your life is like the confidence of a tightrope walker undertaking to tread on the void.

I also gratefully acknowledge the support of the Social Sciences and Humanities Council of Canada, in the form of Insight Grant #43517022.

Never is evil done more thoroughly and gaily than by those who act on moral principle.

Blaise Pascal

Nowadays, everyone is a moralist. Or so it may seem from an hour or two of random browsing on the Internet. While many deplore the news that the Morality Police in Iran continue to arrest and torture women for letting a strand of hair show, Americans eagerly volunteer to serve in moral militias on both sides of America's culture wars. Books are banned, invective replaces argument, speakers are silenced, mobs get professors fired, and just last summer a commentator staged a public burning of a Barbie doll to express his moral outrage at a blockbuster family movie—all in the name of the epic struggle of Good against Evil.

Of course, this moral zeal may be no more genuine than professions of Christian faith in the service of bigotry. In practice, amoralists are not uncommon: we are the ones that refuse to be bullied by the self-righteous. If you are one, I hope merely to encourage you to remain so more thoughtfully.

Meanwhile, in academia, the commitment to morality is no mere pose. A recent biography of the late Derek Parfit (1942–2017), one of the most distinguished and appealingly eccentric philosophers of my generation, describes him as

DOI: 10.4324/9781003278252-1

having been on a 'Mission to save morality . . . from . . . various kinds of skepticism about the existence of objective, normative truths' (Edmonds, 2023). The three volumes of the book Parfit devoted to this mission total 1,980 pages, which is longer than the *Book of Mormon* (530 pages) plus the *Handbook of Scientology* (871 pages) put together. Saving morality turns out to be a long-winded business.

But what if morality didn't deserve to be saved? What if the rules and dictates of morality in the popular mind, as well as philosophers' sophisticated attempts to make sense of it systematically, merely exacerbate the appalling proliferation of abuse on social media, the spread of violence fuelled by political rhetoric, and the inability of politicians to agree on practical solutions to contemporary crises? Drawing up a persuasive indictment along these lines is beyond both my ambition and my powers. My hope in writing this book, more modestly, is to encourage you to see that your 'moral' reasons are not sanctioned by any objective moral facts. And that if you cannot tame your moralistic fervour, you can at least turn it against itself, rather than regard it as a source of smug self-satisfaction.

A SUMMARY ROAD MAP

In the next two chapters, I set the stage by sketching seven strategies that religious leaders and philosophers have adopted for answering the question 'Why should (or should I not) do X?' The answers in question are sometimes understood as explanations, but from the moral point of view they are intended to provide justifications. These comprise first, in Chapter 2, Divine Command Theory, two rather different ways of appealing to nature, Virtue Ethics and Contractarianism; they are followed in Chapter 3 by the main contenders today:

Utilitarian Consequentialism and Kantian Deontology. In addition, Chapter 3 sketches some variants of Noncognitivist views. These attempt to reinterpret moral discourse without being committed to any objective moral facts, and thus might be viewed as a first step towards amoralism.

In Chapter 4, I will suggest that both the popular understanding of morality and the systematic attempts by philosophers to provide it with foundations are unacceptably totalising. They tend to encroach on every aspect of our lives, in ways that none but members of a cult should find attractive.

Chapter 5 delves into some of the complexities of our notion of reasons. In most systems of morality, the assessment of an agent's reasons for acting is a precondition of any judgment of moral responsibility. Understanding what reasons to act are and how we can evaluate them is therefore central to the project of determining the role that morality plays or should play in human life. Adopting a perspective inspired both by common sense and by the 'two systems' or dual processing view of thought and deliberation, we will see that one mode of action explanation appeals to reasons that are largely automatic and unconscious. That level of explanation has the best claim for representing the true causal background of our behaviour. Yet the reasons we make explicit when we attempt to justify what we do are often poor representations of those true reasons. The gap between the two, I shall argue, undermines the project of moral judgment.

Chapter 6 explores the implications of the relation between moral reasons and the natural facts on which they are typically based. Some reasons are said to be moral while others are not. Deciding which reasons are in each category—the problem of demarcation—is a task about which there is little consensus. It will prove to be a recurrent obstacle to the project of making moral theory live up to its universalising ambition. Even if a clean criterion of demarcation were to emerge, we shall see that the relation between non-moral and moral reasons cannot reasonably license the latter to trump the former. For so-called moral reasons do not differ materially from the natural facts that are supposed to ground them. Talk of moral reasons therefore constitutes a kind of double counting that is both fallacious and largely ineffective. The fallacy consists in manufacturing a category of reasons that are 'grounded' in non-moral reasons we already have. The manoeuvre amounts to counting some reasons twice. It is also ineffective, insofar as an agent is unlikely to be swayed by the mere application of the label 'moral' onto a reason the force of which never moved them in the first place.

Chapter 7 focuses on the two most influential traditions of moral philosophy and their preoccupation with foundations. Because foundational principles constitute the ultimate level of justification, no more basic shared criterion exists to arbitrate among all parties. While the resulting philosophical debates display impressive intellectual virtuosity, they present a sorry spectacle of justifying the obvious by question-begging appeals to the abstruse. In addition, the sociological profile of a 'morality' is too often alarmingly similar to that of certain kinds of fanaticism. Fascism, male supremacy, religious ideologies and sexual tyrannies display much the same psychological and social profile as does the consistent imposition of the benign morality you are likely to espouse. Some moralities are just bad, and philosophy's attempts to discriminate them from the 'good' ones are doomed to remain question-begging.

Finally, in Chapter 8, I will address the question of how a life might be lived without morality. In the light of my argument about double counting, the life of an amoralist does not have to be deprived of good reasons, nor must it shun rational deliberation. What difference there is will be attributable to the amoralist's repudiation of the entitlement to indulge in the somewhat nasty emotions that drive moral passion. Those emotions power not just morality and moralising but fanatical cults. Guilt, shame, envy, contempt and resentment typically motivate moral judgments on oneself as well as others, and while they may sometimes function in useful ways, these emotions are in general more noxious than the ills they are claimed to mitigate.

So much for what is to follow. In the present chapter, I begin by clarifying some of the crucial terms that will come into play in the discussions to come. What is morality? Why does it seem to have two opposites, confusingly referred to as *immorality* and *amorality*? What is supposed to be the role of morality in human life, and what about that does an amoralist object to? We shall first look at the notorious question of the 'naturalistic fallacy', which concerns the possibilities of inference from statements of facts to statements of value or 'oughts'. An unbridgeable 'gap' has been held to separate them. With respect to what lies on the latter side of this gap, amoralists take a position sometimes called 'anti-realist' or even 'nihilist'; beyond that common ground, however, there can be differences between different versions of amoralism.

ARE THERE MORAL FACTS?

Informally, we can all think of the oughts, shoulds and don'ts that make up morality as moral rules. Sometimes you feel these rules are pressing on you by the inner voice of conscience. When you fail to heed that voice, you may feel guilt, and you blame others when they fail to heed what you think their conscience should have dictated. We associate morality with duties, obligations and prohibitions that conflict with inclination or desire. And we are easily disposed to believe that the oughts, duties and interdictions of morality are manifestations of the 'moral order'.

That moral order may well seem to be ruled by disinterested, rational principles based on incontrovertible moral facts. Regardless of how you feel on any particular occasion, is it not always true, as sure as the sun will rise tomorrow, that you should be kind, honest, fair? That you should avoid causing harm, do what is right and promote what we all know is good? Affirmative answers to these questions may strike you as obviously true, even when they conflict with your personal preferences. Although the empirical evidence about this is equivocal,[1] many ordinary folks, as well as philosophers— though far from all—are realists about morality. Realism in a given domain is the doctrine that the truths of that domain are independent of anyone's attitudes, emotions or beliefs. Realism is what common sense takes for granted about the truths of mathematics or physics: the facts uncovered in those fields would be what they are even if no one were here to think of them. Similarly, moral realism is the view that moral truths would be what they are even if no one knew or cared.

To be sure, scientific or mathematical facts are formulated in response to questions we ask. We might have asked different questions, and obtained different answers. But that is the only sense in which facts depend on us. Once a question is asked, the answer has nothing to do with what we want or believe. The answers are what they are regardless of how we feel about them. That is not to deny that the facts uncovered by scientific inquiry, like the 'facts' of morality, are often disputed. Indeed, the very existence of a disagreement shows that all parties to the dispute agree that there is an objective fact of the matter. If not, there is nothing to disagree about. Facts should be reflected in opinion, but no 'alternative facts' can be created by opinion. They are *objective*, in a sense that contrasts with the range of states that we recognise as purely *subjective*, such as a preference for some flavour, some colour or some sensation. *De gustibus*, we are often told, *non disputandum*: it is pointless to argue about tastes. For a moral realist, moral values are not matters of taste. That is why they are worth arguing about.

The idea that moral facts are just like physical facts, however, ignores a fundamental difference. The latter are about what *is*, while the former are about *ought*: what I ought to do or not do, what ought to be, what values ought to be promoted or espoused. As David Hume (1711–1776) first pointed out, no purely logical inference is valid from a statement of what *is* to a statement of what *ought* to be. An inference of this kind, however plausible it may seem, commits what is traditionally referred to in philosophy as the *naturalistic fallacy* (see Box #1).

DIRECTION OF FIT

The distinction between factual beliefs on the one hand and wants—in the broadest sense of that word that includes wishes, hopes, desires and cravings—on the other is sometimes formulated in terms of an expression's 'direction of fit'. A factual statement is deemed correct only if its content conforms to or *fits* the way things are in the world. That reflects a minimal definition of truth: *an utterance of 'p' is true if and only if p is the case*. Thus, an expression with *mind-to-world* direction of fit is correct only if the mental state expressed conforms to the way things are in the world, regardless of what we think or want. By contrast, when you utter an *ought*-statement, as in *There ought to be equality of opportunity*, the inequality that exists in the actual world does not invalidate your claim. The point of an ought-statement is precisely to call for the world to conform to what is called for in the utterance, not to conform to the world as it is. Ought-statements therefore have a *world-to-mind* direction of fit. What may obscure this is that value statements in general, such as 'cruelty is contemptible' or 'this Rembrandt painting is beautiful', have a surface grammatical structure that makes them look like factual claims with a mind-to-world direction of fit, but all of them have a world-to-mind direction of fit inasmuch as they implicitly call for the elimination of something that *ought-not-to-be*, or for the promotion or perpetuation of some state of affairs that *should* be promoted or pursued.

BOX #1 THE NATURALISTIC FALLACY

The naturalistic fallacy refers to the mistake of deriving normative statements (what ought to be) from descriptive statements (what is). Although the term was coined by G.E. Moore (1873–1958), the concept was first articulated by the Scottish philosopher David Hume (1711–1776). It never follows logically that just because something is a certain way, it ought to be that way—or any other specific way. This is also referred to as the 'is–ought gap'. For example, consider the statement: 'Animals in nature often kill each other to survive; therefore, it is morally acceptable for humans to kill each other.' This is an example of the naturalistic fallacy because it assumes that the way things occur in nature automatically determines what is morally right or wrong for humans. Moral considerations are not solely determined by observations of the natural world. Additional 'normative' principles and values must determine what ought to be and what ought to be done. Sometimes it may seem obviously correct to infer an ought from an is. But that is always because we tacitly assume an auxiliary premise that just seemed too obvious to mention, but which is itself an ought-statement. For example, the inference from *Doing X will cause someone gratuitous pain* to *You ought not do X* is not valid in logic, but most of us would regard it as reasonable because we take it for granted that one ought never to cause gratuitous harm. When that ought-statement is explicitly included as a premise, we have not committed the naturalistic fallacy because we now have an ought premise to warrant the inference as valid.

This creates a difficulty for the idea that there are objective moral facts. The reason is that it appears to invite us to assent to something very like gobbledygook. What facts in the world as it is can make it *true* that something which *is not true* in the objective world *should be true*? What is there, in other words, that could fit the formula '*p*' is true if and only if p, when the 'fact' p alleged to correspond to a moral proposition is an *ought*? For the point of such a proposition is precisely to call attention to the *non-existence* of p!

IT'S ALL ABOUT REASONS

To lay the ground for answering this question, I will take it for granted that any talk about values or oughts, moral or non-moral, can be translated without loss of meaning into talk about reasons.[2] If I value something, I have a reason to promote or preserve it. If I ought to do something, I have reason to do it. That is true whether we are talking about trivial things or about vitally important ones.

Some philosophers have wanted to draw a barrier between wants and reasons. Some have argued that wanting to do something is not always a reason to do it: it may be simply a fact about myself that may or may not bear on what I *should* do. Others have held that while some wants can provide reasons, that may not be true of all fancies, yearnings, inclinations, preferences, desires, urges, lusts, whims or impulses. The debate can get quite elaborate (Chang 2004; Goldman, 2009). But for my purposes I will ignore nuances and just say that when I ask for your reason, I will accept '*I just wanted to*' as an answer. Since 'want' can refer to anything from gut level lust to a reluctant sense of duty, my reason for doing something issues in a *thinking-I-should* (unless defeated by a stronger contrary reason), whether or not I think of the choice as a moral one.

In any given case, however, you can always ask a further question: why did I want *that*? My answer may lead to more why-questions, until I reach an explanation that satisfies you. Satisfaction is a subjective matter, and someone else might think of further questions still. The hope is that there is some *objective* standard that justifies our shared subjective acceptance of a given explanation. Theories of practical reason, as well as moral theories, attempt to provide just such objective standards.

In the next two chapters, I sketch half a dozen types of answers that have been given to the very general question 'Why should I do (or refrain from doing) X?', paying particular attention to that subclass of reasons for acting that are accorded moral status.

Before I do so, however, I need to address a couple more preliminaries.

DESCRIPTIVE AND NORMATIVE

First, I want to clarify what I am doing when I speak of morality. I am here talking about it in a descriptive way, as opposed to endorsing its normative authority. The aim is to understand the psychological and social mechanisms that underlie judgments, feelings and behaviour that are taken or intended to be expressions of morality. Normative judgments, by contrast, do not describe or explain an agent's mental life, but express endorsements of commands that should be obeyed.

A sentence that begins 'Morality requires that . . .' could be read either way. When uttered by a preacher or a parent, it is most naturally taken as normative, admonishing the hearer to do what morality requires. But when used descriptively, as I shall be doing, or as even a moralist would intend when discussing a morality they do not endorse, it carries no normative force. I might remark, for example, that in a society dominated by an honour code, morality requires that even the slightest affront must be avenged. That assertion does not commit me—or any outsider—to regarding that requirement as binding. It merely asserts a fact about those who do subscribe to an honour code.

TYPES OF OPPOSITES

It also seems appropriate to say a little more about the odd linguistic fact that 'moral' appears to have two opposites. What are the relations among those three words, *morality*, *immorality* and *amorality*?

Both the prefixes *in-* [*im-*] and *a*[*n*] are widely used in English to signal opposites or negation. The latter, being borrowed from the Greek, tends to occur in more recondite scientific or medical terms with other Greek roots: *anaerobic* (able to subsist without oxygen), *aphasia* (loss of speech), *anaesthetic* (causing the absence of sensation).

Sometimes, the *a-* prefix does a more subtle job. It negates not just the positive adjective but the applicability of either it or its contrary. Consider the ancient saying that 'Humans are rational animals'. This dictum is often mistakenly taken to imply that humans are never irrational. Since that proposition is all too obviously false, many have wondered what could have induced anyone to assert it. A charitable principle of interpretation says that if you hear someone saying something absurd, you may have misunderstood them. In this case, the reinterpretation needed is obvious: 'Rational', like 'moral', has two opposites. The ancient dictum does not deny that humans are sometimes irrational. On the contrary, it affirms it: for to be rational is to be the sort of being that can be irrational. The contrast is with those things whose nature precludes any assessment of rationality. Rocks, plants, oysters, insects can't meaningfully be accused of irrationality. They are *arational*—that is, they lie outside the category of things that can be rational or irrational. Similarly, while an *immoral* act or person is *not moral*, they remain the *kind* of act or person that can be described as moral (morally good) or immoral (morally bad). Amorality is the rejection of that very category of appraisal.

What, then, is a judgment in the domain or category of the moral supposed to mean? Much of this book will aim to persuade you that the answer to that question is elusive to the point of uselessness. But we can begin by noting that the domain of the moral comprises two evaluative poles. At the positive pole, a person or action is said to be *moral* if they are deemed to be *good* or *right*. That adjective conveys approval. At the negative pole, captured by the word *immoral*, lies what is *bad* or *wrong*, deserving of disapproval. The moral person does only what they *ought* or are *permitted* to do; the immoral person does what they *ought not* or fails to do what they ought. Both positive and negative judgments are *in the moral domain*.

Both contrast with *amoral* judgments, which involve neither approval nor disapproval. An *amoralist* is one who rejects the relevance of *any* judgment, property or demands in the moral domain.

If we can draw clear boundaries around the domain of the moral, the amoral will comprise everything outside of that. An amoralist is one who regards the moral domain as null, and is thus sometimes aptly referred to as a 'moral nihilist', for they believe that morality is *nihil*—not a thing.

VARIETIES OF AMORALISM

The words 'immoral' and 'amoral' are sometimes confused, and used as a term of condemnation for anything that violates what the speaker regards as moral rules. The previous remarks should make it clear that this is a misuse of the word 'amoral'. An amoralist is not an immoralist. The latter flouts morality, whereas the amoralist insists that there is nothing there to flout or observe. They regard the moral domain as null, and hold that the words 'moral' and 'immoral' don't apply to anything real, any more than *rational* or *irrational* applies to a pebble.

Several positions can be called 'amoralist'. What all deny is the existence of objective moral facts independent of persons' attitudes. Beyond that, amoralist views can differ both in content and in attitude.

One important distinction concerns the interpretation of moral language. Some amoralists take it seriously as making meaningful assertions that might be true or false. The amoralist who takes this approach holds that all such judgments are systematically false. The second approach denies that moral judgments are even *trying* to be true. They belong to an altogether different category, that of 'noncognitive' utterances.

There are two ways in which an utterance might be 'non-cognitive'. It could be nonsense, like a line from Lewis Carroll's 'Jabberwocky' (*'Twas brillig, and the slithy toves / Did gyre and gimble in the wabe . . .'*). But that is not the sense in play here. The other way that an utterance might be classed as noncognitive is illustrated by such uses of language as exclamations, cries of pain or shrieks of joy. That is closer to the sense in which moral language can be claimed to be 'noncognitive'. I will have more to say about it in Chapter 3, and for the moment I set it aside and concentrate on the form of amoralism that regards moral statements as claiming a truth they cannot attain.

That form of amoralism is known as 'Error Theory', an expression associated with Australian philosopher J.L. Mackie (1917–1981). The central claim of Error Theory is simply that there could be no such thing as a moral fact. A fact is the sort of thing that could be discovered, ascertained or disconfirmed; it can serve to explain other states of affairs. But although there are facts about people's moral beliefs, so-called moral facts explain nothing that actually happens; nor does anything count as discovering, ascertaining or disconfirming a moral fact. *That-you-ought-to-do-something* is just too unlike anything else we recognise as a fact. It would seem to follow that all moral claims are simply false (Mackie, 1977).

One way of putting this point is that any moral assertion is false in virtue of the non-existence of moral properties. It is like 'The present King of France is bald', which is false in virtue of the current non-existence of a King of France. In that example, however, notice that to avoid wrongly inferring that the King of France is hirsute, it might feel more natural to say that while 'The present King of France is bald' is clearly not true, it isn't false either. For it does not actually *assert* that there is a current King of France. It merely *presupposes* it. Similarly, the existence of an objective set of moral truths is presupposed by 'Thou shalt not kill' but it is equally presupposed by its contrary, 'Thou *shalt* kill'.[3]

So the central thesis of amoralism might better be stated in a way that directly parallels the corresponding (anti-) theological claim. Any theological proposition presupposes the existence of God; if God does not exist, no theological statement can be either true or false.[4] Similarly, moral claims presuppose the existence of moral truths. If there are no moral truths, then no moral claim is ever true, but neither is it false. The error in moral claims, then, might best be understood as the illusion that moral statements are *either* true or false.

MORALITY FROM THE OUTSIDE

Still, it is all too obvious that people do utter what appear to be intended as true moral statements. From the descriptive point of view, the lack of anything in the world for such statements to be about is irrelevant. For anyone who has concluded that there are no moral facts, the question that arises is what stance to adopt in the face of the *sociological* fact of morality. Here again, the comparison with religion is instructive.

Theistic religion is also a sociological fact; millions of people believe that something objectively exists answering to the conception favoured by their sect. Since that conception differs from one sect to another, and there are thousands of discordant sects, we can be mathematically certain that most of them are wrong about whatever it is they disagree about. We can also note the further sociological fact that antisocial behaviour is no more common in those societies where the majority have given up religion.[5]

Since no society as a whole has yet embraced amoralism, we lack a parallel natural experiment that might test its impact on behaviour. But on at least the anecdotal level, it seems clear that practising amoralists are no more likely than others to do the sorts of things that moralists would deem immoral.[6] The difference between moralists and amoralists is not generally in what they do, but in how self-righteous they feel about it.

Nevertheless, what people believe has real consequences, largely independent of the truth of their beliefs. From the outside, judged by sceptics or agnostics, those consequences may constitute reasons to disabuse believers. Or they might be held, on the contrary, to provide reasons to encourage people to continue believing. The latter stance is sometimes adopted by those sceptics who regard the mass of humans as too weak or ignorant to do without their illusions. Although self-deception is generally deplored, it not infrequently proves encouraging or consoling. In the case of religion, that is especially noticeable when a crushing disaster provides overwhelming evidence against the hypothesis of a benevolent God. For that, paradoxically, seems to motivate believers to reaffirm their faith. 'Religion,' as Karl Marx famously observed, 'is the opium of the people.'

Much the same can be said of belief in morality. As it is all too easy to illustrate, its consequences vary widely among both individuals and societies. Sometimes, agents do or refrain from doing things out of a sense of duty. Some of those things are of a kind you would approve of, while some others, driven by an equally strong sense of duty, do what you may find horrifying. Heinrich Himmler, head of the Nazi SS and in charge of the extermination camps, found the job exceedingly painful. So difficult that he 'suffered a variety of nervous and physical disabilities, including nausea and stomach-convulsions' (Bennett, 1974, p. 129). But he persisted, *because it was his duty* to kill as many Jews as possible.

Not all moralists are as firmly devoted to duty as was Himmler. Like religious leaders, parents and educators do their best, even if they are themselves moral sceptics, to shape their charges' beliefs in such a way as to make them easier to manipulate. Such moral sceptics might be outright amoralists, of the kind called *fictionalists*. They regard morality as a socially useful 'noble lie'. They may even themselves be willing to be self-deceived. They will then behave, and recommend that others behave, *as if* intrinsically normative facts really existed. Fictionalists go along, for the sake of its supposed good consequences, with the fiction that morality exists.

Another variant of amoralism is known as *abolitionism*. As the name implies, it advocates dropping moral talk altogether. Unlike fictionalists, abolitionists do not believe that maintaining belief in the fiction of morality is to be preferred on the whole, even just for those less wise than yourself. We have ceased to debate the fine points of witchcraft detection and punishment set out in the authoritative *Malleus Maleficarum* ('Hammer of Witches') of 1486. There are no witches. Abolitionists urge us, for similar reasons, to give up moral talk altogether. (Garner & Joyce, 2019).

THE SPECTRE OF RELATIVISM

Descriptive accounts of morality cannot but highlight the differences among what people at different times and places take to be morally right or wrong. That deserves comment, because it raises the spectre of relativism. Relativism, the view that what is right and wrong, good or bad, differs from one time and place to another, is commonly dismissed as incoherent. For it entails that one should be tolerant of different moral opinions when they come from different cultures; yet that prescription of tolerance itself seems universal. Most moralists find this unsatisfactory. The amoralist, by contrast, simply avoids the problem by withholding judgments of morality altogether.

Most moralists, and most philosophers bent on the pursuit of True Morality, reject relativism by appealing to the contrast between the descriptive and the normative. They concede the appearance of moral relativity that is conveyed by cultural differences. However, with a few notorious exceptions such as Friedrich Nietzsche (1844–1900) (Nietzsche, 1998 [1887]), they infer only that others have it wrong. A member of one culture may give historical or distant societies a pass because, well, they didn't know any better in those days, or they hadn't yet been civilised. But that just means that others' views need not be taken seriously. In that way, different moralities remain locked in disagreements that are beyond resolution. (See *Gowans, 2021.)

Among rival moralists as among religious sects, there is one proposition that all are prepared to endorse: namely that *all the others are mistaken*. That might induce an agnostic observer to wonder how to determine who is right. Only one can be in possession of the unique truth. Since each is equally confident, an observer must either suspend belief, accept the relativist view that some moral truths are valid only locally after all, or opt for amoralism—the view that no moral judgment has a truth value.

Everyone concedes the importance of local customs: 'When in Rome, do as the Romans.' But the moralist insists on distinguishing merely conventional local norms, such as those of ritual or etiquette, from those of morality. Only the latter hold everywhere and unconditionally, even in those benighted societies that fail to acknowledge them. Properly interpreted, the moralist will protest, 'When in Rome . . .' is itself a universal moral precept, from which the relativity of etiquette follows. To maintain that distinction, however, the moralist requires a principle of demarcation. They need to show that all reasons for action can be sorted into morally significant ones and morally neutral ones. As we shall see, such a principle of demarcation is not easy to formulate. Without one that meets universal approval, every moralist who regards the idea of moral relativity as incoherent must condemn all but what is sanctioned by their own moral code.

The amoral stance I shall be defending in this book repudiates such moral solipsism. It abjures moral condemnation altogether, arrogating neither to itself nor to others the right to make judgments of moral guilt.

WE WERE BRED TO BE MORALISTS

Understood descriptively, the moralistic tendency to blame and punish is unlikely ever to be eliminated altogether from most human beings' enduring dispositions. It is driven by emotions bequeathed to us by natural selection. Evolution, however, does not work solely on our genes. As I will discuss further in the next chapter, cultural change can result in modifications of the living conditions of our species, thus creating new selective forces that affect the very genes that enabled culture. (See Box #2.) And one of the most remarkable features of the joint effects of natural selection and cultural change is that social expectations, norms, and institutions are subject to unpredictably rapid change. In the last century or two, such change has already occurred to an extent that few thinkers committed to the idea of a fixed human nature would likely have imagined. Allow me to mention just two, as spectacular as they were unpredictable, the importance of which is attested by the backlash they have provoked. Both have had vast consequences for general opinions about what attitudes and behaviours are regarded as moral.

- It has been barely more than a century since women won the right to vote. Consider, in the light of women's achievements over just that century, how absurd nineteenth-century assumptions about women's capacities have proved to be. In every domain—athletic, intellectual, artistic, scientific and political—learned opinion agreed with popular prejudice that women were biologically incapable of doing what we now see them doing every day where their capacities are no longer suppressed.

BOX #2 GENE–CULTURE CO-EVOLUTION

The study of gene-culture co-evolution attempts to bring empirical science to bear on the long fruitless nature–nurture debate. It does so by looking at actual influences in both directions, and thus overcoming the appearance of an exclusive dichotomy. Reciprocal interaction between genetic traits and cultural practices within a population over time shapes both trajectories.

Genetic change, whether it is due to purely random genetic drift or results from a process of adaptation, can modify the range of a population's capabilities, and culture can make use of these new capabilities by facilitating the learning and refinement of social practices. Conversely, social practices, possibly facilitated by novel skills, can bring about significant modifications to the environment, and thus affect the selection pressures acting on that population's genome. This is sometimes referred to as Baldwin selection or the Baldwin effect. It explains how some changes seem to result from inheritance of acquired characteristics even when they do not. (See https://en.wikipedia.org/wiki/Baldwin_effect.)

A simple concrete example is provided by the genetically determined ability to digest lactose in adulthood. While this might have arisen by chance in some populations, it favoured the adoption of dairy-farming practices. In turn, those practices provided a selective advantage to individuals in those populations who could process milk.

Another example is provided by genes enabling the development of language. They made possible new forms of social organisation, based on language and tool use, which then provided further selective advantages to genes that enabled more sophisticated cognitive processes.

- Closely related is the increasingly common recognition of the manifest arbitrariness of heteronormative assumptions about erotic relationships. Those standards were inherited from social and economic circumstances now far distant from those now prevalent in Western, educated, industrialised, rich, democratic (WEIRD) regions of the world (Henrich 2020). Mere decades have transformed attitudes to the diversity of sexual orientations and preferences, notably in the acceptance of same-sex marriage in very different countries. Countless works of art and literature, despite the zeal of book banners in States or states where the backlash rages, celebrate queer identities, alternative sexual choices of all kinds and a rich diversity of sexual and gender identities. While none of these is really new, the prevailing morality's attitudes to them have changed profoundly over a mere half century.

The rapidity of these recent social changes, despite the conflicts they have sparked, encourages the hope that if our moralistic impulses cannot be discarded altogether, they might be turned against moralism itself. If we must feel shame or guilt, we should first, I suggest, direct them against our own propensity to feel and ascribe shame and guilt.

IS AMORALITY DEFENSIBLE?

But is amorality not an absurd position? How could it fail to matter whether one is good or evil? Surely no society could subsist unless most of its members approve of good things and disapprove of bad ones, fulfil their moral duties, are motivated by moral values such as kindness, generosity and honesty. Even rule breakers usually acknowledge that the rules exist: such people just tend to make excuses for themselves, while usually insisting that others should conform. There are things we *ought* to do, and things we *ought not* do. We should strive to be good rather than evil, to behave well rather than badly, to act rightly rather than wrongly. At first sight, it seems preposterous to reject the very idea that actions and persons should not be judged as moral or immoral. Far from consisting in a range of judgments that can be ignored, the realm of moral judgment is the most important in the lives of persons.

So it is commonly asserted. Nevertheless, this book will argue, we would be better off if we ceased to worry about morality, and it doesn't mean ceasing to want what we believe to be worth wanting.

THE MANY MEANINGS OF GOOD

A first step on the way to seeing why is to notice that there are many ways of being right or wrong, good or bad. You'd be wrong to believe that 2+2 = 5, or that the author of the *Odyssey* and the *Iliad* was Scottish. You'd be right to check your gas gauge before driving through the desert. Your hat might be the wrong size; a singer might strike the wrong note; your banana could have gone bad; a skilled pickpocket is a bad citizen but might be very good thief. Not all goodness is moral goodness; not every wrong is a moral wrong. So I was misleading when I wrote that a moral person is one who is good, or whose action is right. In fact, that suggestion illustrates its own falsity: it is wrong without being morally wrong. It leaves out the very feature we are seeking: that which demarcates what is moral from what is amoral.

What we are looking for is that special sense of good and bad which parents, religious leaders and philosophers often claim matters more than any other kind of good or bad. Legislators often justify a proposed law by claiming that it promotes morality or discourages immorality. Educators strive to instill moral values in their charges. A good education is one of which the beneficiaries will be morally virtuous. We understand this, among other things, as not causing others gratuitous pain, resisting the temptations of easy pleasures, striving to be kind, fair, generous, honest, rather than cruel, abusive and selfish.

DEFINING MORALITY

All that sounds plausible. It is neatly captured by an influential definition of morality due to Bernard Gert:

> Morality is an informal public system applying to all rational persons, governing behavior that affects others, and includes what are commonly known as the moral rules, ideals, and virtues and has the lessening of evil or harm as its goal.

(Gert, 2005 p. 14)

Gert's definition limits the scope of morality to what affects others. (As we shall see, that condition is not endorsed by all moral philosophers.) Apart from that, it specifies four crucial features of morality: (1) that morality applies to *rational* agents; (2) that it aims at a *goal*, namely the avoidance of harm; (3) that it is *universally* applicable; (4) that it is regarded by those who accept it as *normative*—that is, that it claims a certain authority to govern behaviour.

A definition does not issue commands. It is not itself an ought-statement. These four features, however, are such that anyone who accepts the definition may be led to infer that they are *subject* to certain ought-statements or commands. Such a person, deeming themself rational, must accept some rules as applying to themself. Gert further observes that the rules of morality are those that a rational person would prefer other people to follow: 'morality is best conceived as a guide to behavior that rational persons put forward to govern the behavior of others, whether or not they plan to follow that guide themselves' (Gert 2005, p. 9). This means, for example, that a morality of egoism—do whatever benefits me without regard for the interests of anyone else—is not one that any rational agent could adopt. For if everyone else were consistently selfish, then I should worry that they would avoid harm to themselves but might not care about harm to me.

But couldn't I just adopt egoism for myself and prescribe altruism for all those I come into contact with? Not if I endorse Gert's definition. For its third term—its demand for universal applicability—precludes exempting myself from its normative claims. If I cannot want others to be consistently selfish and believe, with Gert, in the universality of moral rules, then I must, on pain of inconsistency, consider myself bound by those rules as well.

In this way, then, although the definition presents itself as purely descriptive, its acceptance by any member of the community would in fact require the acceptance of the commands entailed by the goal it specifies, of avoiding harm or evil.

We will have occasion, in the subsequent chapters, to discuss this crucial condition of universality. We will also consider what it could mean for there to be a set of rules or commands that we *must* obey even in the absence of any authority, divine or human, by which such rules are legitimately promulgated. For the moment, let us turn to the question of how the goal of 'lessening harm or evil' might best be pursued, and how it can answer the question of demarcating the peculiar use of words such as good and bad that count as moral as opposed to those that do not.

To do this, we could hardly do better than to follow the lead of some of the world's great thinkers. They have elaborated theories intended to derive, from that vague goal or from other considerations deemed even more fundamental, the rules that morality imposes.

Four answers to why-questions

Everyone calls barbaric whatever customs aren't their own.
Michel de Montaigne

As I noted in the previous chapter, I will take for granted that any talk about moral or nonmoral values, and any talk about what we ought to do, can be translated without loss into talk about reasons. Whenever we *ought* to do (or think, or feel) something, we have a *reason* to do (or think, or feel) it. If challenged, we will usually attempt to adduce justifications in the form of further reasons, perhaps regarded as more basic. In the case of moral reasons, the resulting play of challenge and response in search of ever more basic reasons has taken thinkers onto a quest for 'foundations'. Such foundations would consist in reasons so basic and so compelling that they neither require nor admit of further justification.

This quest has led to a variety of kinds of ultimate reasons. In this chapter and the next, I propose to look briefly at six such kinds of reasons: *Divine Command Theory*, *Nature and Natural Law*, *Virtue Ethics*, *Contractarianism*, *Utilitarianism* and *Deontology*. Chapter 3 will also look at a seventh, noncognitive alternative: *Emotionism*, which proceeds by reinterpreting moral judgments not as claiming factual truth at all, but rather as expressing *attitudes* to natural facts. Noncognitive 'metaethical' views— theories about the meanings of moral terms—are actually

DOI: 10.4324/9781003278252-2

already a step closer to amoralism. This chapter will rehearse some unoriginal reasons for rejecting each of the first four, and I shall have little to say about them in the sequel.

DIVINE COMMAND THEORY

Theistic religion is in decline in many countries. Nevertheless, many people, especially in the USA, still regard God's command as the indispensable ultimate guide to what is right and good—and believe that atheists, for that reason, are not to be trusted (Gervais, 2014).

On the face of it, this makes a lot of sense. It explains that morality issues imperatives: *Thou shalt do this; Thou shalt not do that.* This is because God is typically conceived as a superior agent, omnipotent, omniscient and perfectly benevolent, whose nature entails the authority to issue inescapable commands. On the face of it, this answer to the question of ultimate justification is satisfying, for in the absence of such an agent, the origin of commands-without-a-commander is mysterious. As we shall see, that is precisely the position that secular systems of morality are in. They posit and attempt to justify systems of prohibitions and duties that look like commands, and are expected to be obeyed as if they were authoritative commands, but are, as it were, hanging in the sky, deprived of a commander, like the grin of the Cheshire cat or Magritte's *Castle of the Pyrenees.*[1]

On the other hand, the theory requires us to take on a load of auxiliary hypotheses: notably that there is a God; that God cares about what we do; and that we can discover what God's commands actually are. All three assumptions are notoriously dubious. Different societies or sects have disagreed, passionately enough to motivate mutual slaughter, about the nature of God, the tenor of his commands and the channels through which we come to know them.

If some religion's tenets are all true, every other religion holding incompatible beliefs must be false. Since God would presumably underwrite all answers to all questions, there would be a religious Truth, some of which would consist in moral facts, stemming from imperatives valid absolutely, issued by the highest of conceivable authorities. There is no objective way, however, to discern which is the True Religion. Hence, the reliability of what appears to be a divine command cannot be high.

Research suggests that ordinary people commonly feel both guided and motivated by the thought that what they regard as right is sanctioned by the divinity (Gervais, 2014). In practice, what anyone regards as divinely commanded depends on what is generally taken to be morally right in the community.

There are always dissenters, however. Their mere existence, in or outside of any given community, shows that what is generally taken to be right can be doubted. Different gods contradict one another, and contradictory beliefs can't all be true. Despite its wide acceptance, therefore, most philosophers have concluded that the Divine Command Theory of morality cannot provide a rationally justifiable foundation for morality.

The Euthyphro dilemma

Divine Command Theory raises a further problem, which has bequeathed an intriguing insight to recent thinking about morality. It comes from a puzzle posed by Socrates. In an eponymous Platonic dialogue, the young Euthyphro claims to be doing something pious in taking his father to court for the murder of a slave. Socrates is uninterested in the murder itself. Instead, he demands that Euthyphro define the 'pious'. Euthyphro replies that it is 'what pleases the gods'. Socrates follows up: Are the gods pleased *because* something is pious? Or is anything pious *because* it pleases them? (Plato, 1997a).

In the first case, we have not actually said anything about the nature of the pious. We have learned no more about it than 'Ambrosia is what the gods drink' would tell us about the chemical composition of ambrosia. The pious, like ambrosia, would be what it is even if the gods didn't happen to favour it. In the latter case, Euthyphro's statement amounts to a synonym for 'the pious'. It entails that any action liked by the gods is pious, regardless of any other characteristic.

This second answer, assuming piety implies moral goodness, can seem paradoxical. Adherents of most faiths would also have strong intuitions about the wrongness of, say, murdering innocent children. But if they accept the second prong of Euthyphro's dilemma, they would have to agree that if God ordered the murder of children, that would suffice to make it right. For that reason, theologians have toiled to explain away murders commanded by God, such as Abraham's test of faith (*Genesis* 22), when he was ordered to sacrifice his own son, or when God orders the massacre of whole populations (e.g. *Deuteronomy* 20:16–18).[2]

Recent moral thinking, having discarded theology, has inherited this question in a slightly different form. It concerns ordinary judgments made by human agents, not gods, and it goes like this. When you assert that something is morally good, is there some objective fact of morality that justifies that assertion? Or does judging something to be good just express your approval, perhaps reflecting a consensus in your social group?

This question exposes a deep problem faced by any claim of objectivity for moral principles. The endorsement or rejection of a moral principle is closely associated with the

sentiment of approval or disapproval. If a given moral judgment is objectively correct, that association between the
rightness of the principle and your approving attitude must
be contingent. The sentiment of approval may at least sometimes be misplaced. In the absence of compelling evidence
for an objective and authoritative outside source, the dictates
of morality remain impossible to verify. They might derive
from nothing beyond each individual's conviction. Faced
with disagreement, believers can only reiterate their mutual
question-begging. As we shall see in Chapter 3, however,
the second, subjective, answer to the question of justification
can motivate a 'noncognitive' construal of moral statements
that some philosophers have used to construct a conception
of morality grounded in human attitudes rather than objective facts.

NATURE AND NATURAL LAW

In the absence of a God empowered to issue absolutely
authoritative commands, many philosophers have urged that
we regard Nature as the best guide to how to live. 'Follow
Nature' is a precept propounded by wisdom traditions in
several cultures, including the Chinese and the Stoics of
Ancient Greece and Rome. In contemporary thinking, it has
taken two very different forms. One takes its inspiration from
the modern scientific understanding of evolution by natural
selection. The other starts with a conception of nature that
retains essential ties to the idea of a Creator. The latter idea
is known as Natural Law Theory. It goes back to Thomas
Aquinas (1225–1274), who in turn borrowed much from
Aristotle, and it still forms the core of the moral teachings of
the Roman Catholic Church.[3] I turn to this first.

Natural Law Theory

Aristotle taught that every living thing strives to attain its own end. Sometimes it doesn't succeed, but in some sense it *should* have succeeded. To discover what nature intends, we need to look to 'what happens always or for the most part' (Aristotle, 1984, pp. 1026b27–31). Conforming to those natural ends will ensure that we are doing what is right; going against natural law will be morally wrong.

Despite its plausible premise and vast following in the Catholic faith and beyond, this idea cannot function as a guide to what is right and good. The reasons are of two kinds.

The first is that there is nothing about what is most frequent that warrants that it is good. That also constitutes a fatal flaw of the modern variant of naturalistic ethics, discussed in the next section, where I will say more about it. The second reason is specific to Natural Law Theory. It consists in the radical incompatibility between evolutionary theory and Natural Law Theory's presupposition that 'nature intends' anything at all.

Nature appears steeped in teleology. We can often agree about what seems to be the function of an organ. The heart's function is to circulate the blood; the lungs' is to supply the blood with oxygen. Biological functions can be identified with the characteristic processes that explain the existence and structure of the organs in question. The heart and the lungs were formed and preserved by natural selection because the effects they produced contributed to the success of the organisms in which they were found.[4] But nature, unlike God, has no intentions; there is no such thing as a *mistake* of nature, and there is therefore no principled way to make the distinction between what nature intends and what just happens.

Natural Law Theory's bait-and-switch

In fact, Natural Law Theory is a bait-and-switch proposition, resting on ambiguities in the meanings of both 'nature' and 'law'. We sometimes use the words 'nature' or 'natural' in contrast to 'artificial' or 'human made'. In that sense, green-grocers boast of stocking only natural products, meaning ones that exclude certain 'artificial' additives or cultivation methods. But an equally common use of the term 'nature' refers to everything that exists in the actual world. That excludes supernatural intervention, but includes anything made by humans or even by robots.

'Law' is also ambiguous. In one sense, it refers to physically necessary correlations discovered by empirical science, such as the laws of motion or gravitation. In another sense, it refers to rules created by legislation. The latter, but not the former, can be infringed. The law of gravity doesn't tell you that you shouldn't levitate, but that you cannot; laws governing private property do not say you cannot steal, but only that you should not.

Now here is the bait-and-switch. Natural Law Theory begins with the promise of looking to nature, as if it were seeking to uncover laws of nature as understood in science. But it then interprets what is allegedly discovered as what nature intends, but sometimes fails to achieve. It takes seriously Aristotle's idea that some of the things that occur in nature can be dismissed as nature's mistakes. If what nature intends is what happens 'always or for the most part', any exceptions are not treated as falsifying the putative law, as they would be in science. Instead, they are condemned as *morally wrong*.

That is actually a double bait-and-switch: bearing on both 'nature' and 'law'. The first switch is from the descriptive conception of nature to a normative conception, dismissing some of what happens as having gone wrong. Second, it switches from the descriptive perspective associated with scientific laws to the legislative sense of 'law'. The exception is an infringement, deserving of blame or punishment.

If we could assume, with Aristotle, that species remain unchanged forever, it would make sense to consider some events or forms of existence as exceptions, without any effect on the normal future course of things. Even then, it is an unwarranted further leap to claim that what is exceptional is thereby also bad or blameable. That further leap is enthusiastically taken by moralists such as Aquinas, as well as Kant, who, for example, regards any sexual practices that transgress the narrow boundaries of heterosexual marital intercourse as not only unnatural but *contra naturam*, *against* nature, and to be morally condemned.

More generally, as we shall shortly see, what happens always or for the most part is not necessarily better than what happens rarely. We need only glance at the obvious fact that we often regard exceptional people as highly admirable, when their difference happens to be one we prize: intelligence, for example, or athletic prowess.

More generally, in the light of evolution, it makes no sense to regard what is rare as intrinsically less valuable than what is common. Reflect on the long lineage from our most distant unicellular ancestors to present-day *Homo sapiens*. At every stage in that lineage where some small change brought an ancestor closer in some tiny way to our present nature, that ancestor must necessarily have been unique: different from all their predecessors and peers, in just that feature that brought them closer to you and me.

Evolutionary Ethics

The contemporary variant of the counsel to 'follow nature' looks to evolution by natural selection for inspiration, while avoiding some of the mistakes of Natural Law Theory.

Current versions of Evolutionary Ethics do not take natural selection directly as a model for understanding what might be meant by 'good' or 'right'. The interpretation of the phrase 'survival of the fittest' that was once used to justify laissez-faire capitalism is no longer in vogue. Rather, taking for granted that the dispositions and capacities that natural selection has bequeathed us have allowed our species to thrive, defenders of Evolutionary Ethics attempt to identify those winning strategies. To understand what is proposed, let me first very briefly recall the features of the theory of evolution by natural selection on which it is based.

The fundamental idea is as simple as it is powerful. It applies, beyond biology, to any historical or psychological process defined by just three conditions. First, some domain of organisms (or artefacts, or behaviours) offers a diversity of types. Second, types get preserved or copied with very high (though not perfect) accuracy. Third, the space or 'niche' available to the various types in that domain is limited in capacity. It is more favourable to some types than to others. As a result, some types perpetuate themselves better. By that mechanism, natural selection has honed the capacities of every surviving species to deal successfully with their environment.

Some thinkers have argued that our very survival as a social species shows that evolution has adapted our natural dispositions to social life. Amoralists can readily agree. The 'error theorist' John Mackie (1977), whom we met in the previous chapter, takes something like this position, as does Richard Joyce, who, while identifying as an amoralist, has written extensively about the evolution of morality (Joyce, 2006, 2019). The way our social nature has evolved to favour certain ways of interacting is a legitimate topic of empirical inquiry. It can lead us to a descriptive thesis from which we might infer that many of our natural dispositions—our capacity to care for children and more generally to care about others, to avoid causing harm, to resent unfairness—are conducive to social harmony. But that conclusion is still one step away from endorsing the dispositions that natural selection has endowed us with. There are two reasons for this. The first is that such an endorsement by any individual subject presupposes that they *want* to live in a harmonious social environment. (Some may just prefer chaos.) The second, even more important reason, is that natural selection has also endowed us with dispositions that impair rather than promote social harmony, such as the capacity to become murderously jealous, enraged or cruel.

Design without designer

Natural selection does explain the existence of organisms that appear to be cunningly designed. It explains design without recourse to a designer. (But not without a good deal of waste, we might note, since an estimated 99.9% of all species are extinct. Evolution's 'design' is not all *that* smart.) Both cats and mice thrive because natural selection has ensured that most cats can run fast enough to catch *some* mice, and most mice can run fast enough to outrun *most* cats.

Natural selection thus comes to look like Providence. When it works, it results, to take but one example, in the survival in equilibrium of both prey and predator. Similarly, the nature of *Homo sapiens* has been honed to its present shape by the collaborative forces of genetic and cultural evolution. So it might seem plausible to surmise that after 500 million years of improvements, evolution has had time to do a pretty good job. Shouldn't we be close to perfect? Or at least, we must be as fit as we need to be to thrive in our world as it is. This should be the case especially for the most *normal* members of our species: those whose traits are most widely shared and hence presumably proved equal to the most trials. Following this line of reasoning, a Naturalist morality might conclude that whatever is most normal is most moral.

Unfortunately, however, this notion of normality manifests some serious misunderstandings. For several reasons, natural selection does not guarantee that what is statistically most frequent is optimal. I will sketch four major reasons for this: first, adaptation is always falling behind; second, evolution can never redesign anything by starting over from scratch; third, fitness is sometimes 'frequency-dependent'; and fourth, there is an abyss between normality and normativity.

ADAPTATION CAN NEVER CATCH UP

The first reason is the most obvious: adaptation is a race against change, and necessarily always falls behind. Even if we can imagine a trait becoming dominant as a result of natural selection in a stable environment, any change in that environment may find those best adapted to it now at a disadvantage. That makes it unlikely that a specific type or trait might be remain perfectly adapted over a long stretch in a changing environment.

EVOLUTION IS TINKERING

Natural selection, as the French geneticist François Jacob (1920–2013) pointed out, is a 'bricoleur', a tinkerer (Jacob, 1976). It can work only on what is already there. No organism is ever redesigned from scratch. What is 'selected', moreover, never needs to be perfect: it needs only to be less bad than the competing alternatives. (As the lion starts chasing the two hunters, one of them exclaims, 'We can never outrun it!' And the other, leaping ahead, replies, 'I only have to outrun *you*!'). Organisms are riddled with 'kluges': awkward workarounds of inept design. An often-mentioned example is the proximity of the breathing tube to the swallowing tube—resulting in thousands of lives lost to choking. Another example is the blind spot in our eyes that results from the bizarre layout of our optical fibres. As they enter the eye and distribute themselves over the retina, they turn around and face backwards, thus depriving their entry point of receptors. Yet another is the pain and not infrequently lethal character of parturition which, if it had resulted from intelligent design, could only be attributed to a sadistic designer.

In short, even the astonishing ingenuity of evolution is in no way bound to come up with the best possible solutions. Nature has no need to aim for the best, and doesn't get rid of old and now useless organs unless they have become seriously harmful. Even when harmless, though, they may be taking up space and resources that a freshly designed version could have put to better use. Familiar examples are wings in flightless birds, vestigial organs like legs in snakes, or the human vermiform appendix.

Only marginally less obvious is natural selection's shaping of the emotional and behavioural dispositions that rule moral life. To the extent that such dispositions are likely to have changed more slowly than the conditions to which they were originally attuned, we should expect that some of them, while they may have served our ancestors well enough in previous ages, no longer promote social harmony or individual happiness. Such, we might surmise, are dispositions to rape, to endure destructive emotions like jealousy, tribal hatred or easily triggered lethal aggression. And, if the arguments of this book carry weight, the 'moral' emotions of guilt, shame, resentment and blame.

FREQUENCY-DEPENDENT FITNESS

When alleles (alternative genes at a single location) compete for reproductive success, their comparative fitness is sometimes relative to their own frequency in the population. In such cases, there is no unconditionally 'best' allele. A well-known model for this idea, borrowed from game theory (*Alexander, 2020), is due to John Maynard Smith (1920–2004). He asks us to consider a population consisting of 'Doves' and 'Hawks', committed to different strategies when competing for any resource. Hawks are always ready to fight to the death; Doves will retreat without a fight. Thus, Doves will always lose out to Hawks, but need never be seriously hurt (Maynard Smith, 1984).

In a population consisting almost only of Hawks, Doves have the advantage. Hawks will often be seriously wounded or killed in combat; Doves, though hungry, survive to try again. As soon as Doves become too numerous, however, Hawks gain the upper hand: for now that more of their confrontations are with Doves, Hawks are better placed to monopolise resources. We can expect an oscillation about an equilibrium point in the proportion of Hawks to Doves. Evolutionary biologists refer to this as an 'Evolutionarily Stable Strategy' (ESS).

Note that the ESS does not necessarily refer to a ratio of individual Doves to Hawks. A single individual could play either role. The equilibrium holds over events involving the alternative strategies, not over individuals. It reflects the number of

Why It's OK to Be Amoral

occasions on which some individual adopts a Dove strategy, in relation to the number of occasions in which some individual adopts a Hawk strategy.

Here is one way this might apply to an actual human society. Let us adopt a common definition of a psychopath as a person who is emotionally insensitive to the plight of others. There are persons who meet that definition, and whose insensitivity extends even to their own suffering in the future. This manifests itself in their lack of physiological fear responses when confronted with imminent pain.

Now, we might think it best for any society not to harbour any psychopaths. But the proportion of psychopaths, like that of Hawks in the thought experiment envisaged by Maynard Smith, might constitute an ESS. In a community made up exclusively of psychopaths, they would, like the Hawks of the fable, promote their own extinction. For their mutual encounters will prove fatal to at least one participant almost every time. In a community of non-psychopaths, by contrast, no conflicts will be lethal, since, like Doves, non-psychopaths are more likely to live and let live. In the community where both types are present, there will develop an ESS, the exact location of which between the two extremes will depend on all kinds of external conditions. In actual fact, our society seems to be of just that sort (Hare & Babiak, 2006). If the current frequency of psychopathy—estimated at somewhere between 1% and 2%—represents an ESS, that would mean that in the *natural* or *normal* situation for a human population, natural selection will never eliminate psychopaths altogether.

The lesson to retain is that there is no such thing as a *best* disposition or strategy guaranteed by natural selection. There are often just alternative strategies in equilibrium, at a point determined by the nature and frequencies of gains and losses for each strategy under prevailing conditions. Even more disconcerting, perhaps, is a second lesson, which is that natural selection may never eliminate what we regard as bad outcomes. If we think of Doves and Hawks as alternative forms of life, common sense might incline us to regard Doves as the nice guys, and Hawks as nasty. An ESS will preserve both; only the ratio between them will vary.

The previous example is of a case where evolution preserves something undesirable. There are also cases where frequency-dependent fitness determines a point of equilibrium that is optimal for the population as a whole. The balance between rival policies of *exploration* and *exploitation* is a good example. It arises in domains as distant from one another as insect foraging and scientific research. If every ant espoused a single foraging strategy, or if every scientist followed the same basic research paradigm, that would seem highly efficient for a while, but without exploration of other terrains or paradigms, the resource thus exploited will sooner or later be exhausted. *Some* foragers, or researchers, should devote themselves to randomised or eccentric searches. But again, if too many do so, the existing methods will remain underused. Wherever equilibrium may settle, each strategy seems good in itself, and the ratio between them is also good. But it still makes no sense to think of one type or strategy as *the Best*.[5]

NORMALITY VERSUS NORMATIVITY

In both Natural Law Theory and Evolutionary Ethics, the concept of normality played an important role. The word is a tricky one that can be used in different ways. In one use, it has a purely descriptive meaning, equivalent to the more specific 'statistical normality', which somewhat vaguely refers to the middle region, or mode, of a bell curve representing the 'normal' distribution of a property among a set of items. Height, for example is distributed among people in such a way that very few are very short or very tall; as we get closer to the middle of the curve, there are more people of any given height. The shape of the bell can be steeper or flatter, and it can be skewed in various ways, but most people are going to be somewhere around the middle of most distributions. Most people are average.

This use of 'normal' is purely descriptive. The thought too easily creeps in, however, that in most respects (save things like IQ or athletic prowess), it is best to be 'like other people', so that being average is 'normal' and therefore good. In biology, where it is very natural to think in teleological terms, it seems plausible to assume that the statistically normal is functionally normal, or, in other words, that most things are as they should be.

Nevertheless, there is an important reason to downplay the normative role of the statistical concept of biological normality. It is that evolution could never have taken place had all members of any population been normal. Think once again of that ancestor of yours or mine, as remote as you like before any counted as human. That ancestor's genome differed from that of its parent in some way that made it just slightly more like you and me. You have millions of such ancestors. Each, by definition, must have been unique among its kind— a freak. Once we take stock of that undeniable fact, should we not value freaks among us, above all mere 'normals'? For only freaks can possibly have a chance, however remote, of improving our genetic legacy.

Much the same is true of cultural evolution. Most Europeans regard the abolition of slavery and gladiatorial combat as 'moral progress' achieved since the heyday of the Roman empire.

And many now think we have yet to make more changes, by abolishing such practices as eating animals. But each of these opinions began as (statistically) highly abnormal.

In short, any change regarded as progressive, judged by any standard of 'progress' you might choose, involves some individual or group coming to believe something nobody else believed. The freak theory of progress holds for societies as well as biological organisms.

So much, then, for the idea that as products of natural selection we should endorse as normative what seems most frequent either by nature or convention. Neither the 'natural' nor the 'normal' can give us any insight into what we should want.[6]

VIRTUE ETHICS

'Virtue Ethics' refers to a recent revival of the Aristotelian point of view. Unlike Natural Law Theory, it is not committed to arbitrary distinctions based on quasi-theological prejudices. It has been favoured by moral philosophers who have felt dissatisfied with Utilitarianism and Deontology, the moral (or strictly 'metaethical') theories that still dominate the field. Both of these theories, as I shall be arguing in Chapter 4, have tended to generate excessively rigid rules ill-suited to the complex messiness of human affairs.

For much of this resistance, feminist philosophers and psychologists are especially to be credited. The psychologist Carol Gilligan, in an influential book published in 1982, noted that theories of development seemed to regard rigid Kantian Deontology as marking the highest form of moral development (Gilligan, 1982; Noddings, 1983). Kantian Deontology seemed to reflect men's point of view more often than women's, a fact that was too easily taken to indicate moral deficiency in women, rather than philosophers' and psychologists' prejudices. It also tended to minimise the role in human thriving of personal relationships, and neglect individual differences. It failed to take into account the origin of some gender differences in oppressive conditions endured by women and other vulnerable groups. This line of thought has become a thriving branch of moral philosophy (*Norlock, 2019). But from the perspective developed in this book, it is just one more reason to cast doubt on the project of demarcating morality.

Virtue Ethics aims to follow Aristotle's wise advice not to strive for standards of precision unwarranted by the nature of our inquiry. Its advocates have urged us to ask not 'What must I do or refrain from?' but rather 'What sort of person should I be?' It recommends attending to issues of character rather than universal rules or prohibitions. Character is best understood as embodied in specific people who are worthy of being regarded as models. The Ancient Greeks referred to such a person as *kalos k'agathos*, roughly 'handsome and good'; the Chinese term was *junzi*, literally 'noble son'. In English, it is often translated 'gentleman', a term that is loaded with sexist and class prejudice (nicely illustrated by a saying familiar in my English childhood that 'a gentleman is someone who is never rude unless he wants to be'[7]), but it is generally taken to refer to a person who embodies moral goodness. Moral goodness is then taken to consist in the possession of traditional virtues, such as kindness, modesty, courage, prudence, generosity, justice. Such virtues are rooted in the natural capabilities of persons, but they require cultivation by an education designed to inculcate good habits of behaviour.

In aid of cultivating the right character, advocates of Virtue Ethics also like to refer to the *phronimos*, the person of practical wisdom. The *phronimos* delivers correct judgments in every case, without even needing, or indeed being capable of formulating, any explicit method that has led them to it. Like Confucius at age 70, who claimed to have attained the capacity to 'follow my heart's desire without overstepping the boundaries of what was right', the *phronimos* has become an oracle who cannot be wrong but also cannot explain how to get there. It leaves it up to each of us to pick the paragon we aspire to emulate; and each agent's choice might itself start a chain of debate in need of oracular resolution.

The general formula, admittedly, need not be interpreted rigidly. It sports a number of variants. There is nothing in the idea of virtue that necessarily sets narrow limits on the range of characteristics that may be counted as such. Indeed, one advantage of ideals of virtues over specific rules of conduct is vagueness. The emulation of admirable models might be interpreted so broadly as to carry little commitment to anything specific. When so interpreted, it allows for many ways of being human equally worth pursuing.

The supposed unity of the virtues

Some philosophers, starting with Plato and including some among our own contemporaries who want to centre the role of virtue in ethics, have held that while kindness, courage, modesty, justice and other virtues are different, they are actually all manifestations of a single comprehensive virtue. That view enjoys little support from either common sense or philosophers, who more plausibly regard virtues as modular. Just as one person might be highly talented for playing the piano but hopeless at spelling, or formidable as a basketball player but poor at mathematics, so a person might be courageous but cheat on their taxes, or scrupulously honest but overbearing and unkind. Nevertheless, there remains a wide-spread assumption among ordinary people in America that someone whose behaviour is morally wrong could not possibly exemplify *any* virtue. Some readers may recall that after the terrorist attacks of 11 September 2001, a TV commentator was forced to issue an abject apology. He had suggested that the terrorists, however vile their motives, could not specifically be charged with cowardice, since their attack involved the deliberate planning of their own violent death.

Rather than thinking of virtue as something that is wholly embodied in certain model persons whom we should all emulate, one might take Virtue Ethics as a guide to what we should avoid. Anti-virtues would be tendencies to act in ways that are widely thought to be deplorable in character or motivation. Borrowing a list from Rosalind Hursthouse, we might strive to avoid

> courses of action that would be irresponsible, feckless, lazy, inconsiderate, uncooperative, harsh, intolerant, selfish, mercenary, indiscreet, tactless, arrogant, unsympathetic, cold, incautious, unenterprising, pusillanimous, feeble, presumptuous, rude, hypocritical, self-indulgent, materialistic, grasping, short-sighted, vindictive, calculating, ungrateful, grudging, brutal, profligate, disloyal, and on and on.
>
> (*Hursthouse & Pettigrove, 2018)

All of these characterisations provide reasons to refrain, but they raise again the problem of demarcation. It is quite unclear which of them should be deemed immoral and which are otherwise undesirable. Why bother to make the distinction? It remains difficult to insist that there is something highly specific about the moral domain, or at least about moral virtues in particular, that makes moral virtues and vices distinct from other sorts of talents, dispositions to excellence or their corresponding failures.

The regressive thrust of Virtue Ethics

Here is another complaint against Virtue Ethics. Too much reliance on what is conventionally regarded as an ideally virtuous person on whom we should model ourselves is liable to stifle social criticism. Too many people, even now, are apt to endorse the kind of definition offered to Socrates by Meno in the dialogue that bears his name:

> The virtue of a man [is to] know how to administer the state, and in the administration of it to benefit his friends and harm his enemies; and he must also be careful not to suffer harm himself. A woman's virtue . . . is to order her house, and keep what is indoors, and obey her husband.
> (Plato, 1997b, 71e2–4)

Given the Aristotelian perspective that grounds it, Virtue Ethics assumes that we can specify *a* human nature, of which the proper expression can be determined and emulated. Deviations from that paradigm are to be deplored as failing to recognise the inherent 'purposes' of human life. Although it does not endorse the primacy of the average, since the Virtuous Person is actually seldom encountered, the version most closely identified with Aristotle still owes too much to the quasi-naturalistic theories criticised above, and seems to presuppose that there is some best way to be human.

Virtue Ethics is both too rigid and too vague

Thus, Virtue Ethics seems uncomfortably poised between a version that imposes on all an excessively uniform model of the good life and another that is too vague to do more than label a set of intuitions, which differ from one geographical or historical context to another.

While it might seem laudable and indeed inevitable to strive to emulate those we admire, that platitude does both too much and too little to count as a theory of morality. It does too much, in that the cultivation of well-established, recognised models of excellence may stifle experiments in living. That seems particularly regrettable in an age where unprecedented developments in technology are removing constraints and reconfiguring life possibilities available to individuals. But it also does too little, in that its more flexible variants can gives us little guidance. If we no longer assume that the models deemed worthy in the past must remain so forever, it gives us no systematic way to select new ideals and forms of life.

All in all, the intentions of Virtue Ethics are laudable. For it recognises a far broader range of virtues than merely 'moral' ones. It embraces the aesthetic, epistemic, perhaps even affective virtues, while also rejecting dogmatic and totalising systems. Which amounts to saying that it is worth adopting precisely insofar as it is a form of amoralism. I shall say no more about it.

CONTRACTARIANISM

This fourth approach to answering the justification question is more concerned with political institutions than with individual morality. I therefore discuss it only briefly.[8]

It is once again with Plato that the key idea of Contractarianism originated. It begins with the observation that human beings in isolation are pathetically feeble. By collaborating, however, any member of a society can aspire to far more ambitious goals, and achieve them more efficiently. But collaboration inevitably gives rise to the temptation of 'free riding', taking advantage of the collective effort while shirking from one's own contribution. The basic problem confronted by any social organism is that of motivating individuals to shun free riding.

Thomas Hobbes (1588–1679), the greatest historical exponent of a contractarian theory, took a pessimistic view of this problem. He concluded that it could be solved only by a 'covenant', or agreement, in which members of a community entrust a dictator with the absolute power to enforce collaboration. Psychologically realistic observers of human behaviour have been more sanguine. Altruistic behaviour, aimed at securing some advantage for another even at the cost of one's own, is a surprisingly common feature of social interaction. That suggests that a partial solution lies in our biological heritage. Clearly, however, our genetic endowment does not consist in the quasi-mechanical altruism displayed by social insects. At best, our genes can provide only the means for groups of humans to entrain and reward prosocial dispositions.

No one believes that any such agreement as Hobbes's 'covenant' actually existed at the origin of human social life. Regardless of how it actually came about, however, an institution might be regarded as justified if it is of a kind that could have been agreed on for mutual advantage.

That suggests a thought experiment: What would a group of reasonable agents be expected to agree on? In Hobbes's version of this idea, the agreement was not about the institutions themselves, but rather about the need for an absolute sovereign to set up, dictate and enforce the rules governing society. In the twentieth century, John Rawls (1921–2002) endeavoured to perfect the test envisaged by such a fictionalist version of Contractarianism. He suggested imposing certain constraints on the members of the constitutional assembly charged with formulating the agreement. The point of the constraints is to secure impartiality in every member of the envisaged constitutional assembly (Rawls, 1977).

Any actual group charged with setting out a constitution—in the French or American revolutions, for example—would comprise individuals who have interests of their own. These interests may skew their sense of fairness. Consequently, the main constraint that Rawls's proposal involves is a 'Veil of Ignorance' that precludes any knowledge of the participants' future role or status in the institutions being constructed. It is then inferred that no constitutional assembly, when protected by the Veil of Ignorance, would ever set up a slave society. For any participant would be deterred from endorsing such a proposal by the mere possibility that, once the veil is lifted, they might find themself a slave.

In the form envisaged by Rawls, this idea focuses especially on social and political institutions rather than moral rules governing individual behaviour. It is therefore only of marginal relevance to the debate between moralism and amorality, since it implies specific rules of conduct only insofar as those might be derived from one's acceptance of prevailing institutions. But since none of us is actually party to the fictional constitutional assembly, it is not clear to what extent any one member of an existing society should feel bound to obey its dictates. Just as moral rules are not the same as legal ones, so moral reasoning is not the same as legal reasoning.

Indeed, there is a long history of civil disobedience, which violates laws on the basis of moral scruple.

Some philosophers, however, such as David Gauthier (1932–2023), have adapted the core idea of Contractarianism in order to make it applicable to the informal institutions of morality. A contractarian morality would be one grounded in principles and rules that reasonable people might agree on, with a view to curbing any agent's pursuit of self-interest when a sacrifice is required to serve communal and long-term interests (Gauthier, 1987).

Unsurprisingly, contractarian theory has been met with objections. I mention only one.

Recall the key device used by Rawls to secure the impartiality of his fictional contractors. The Veil of Ignorance is supposed to conceal from each member of the fictional constituent assembly the status they will have in the society to which their rules will apply. Without knowing in advance whether I shall be a master or a slave, a man or woman, weak or strong, smart or stupid, I will be more likely to want fairness for everyone. For if the blueprint puts some at a severe disadvantage, I might turn out to be one of those. (Rawls or Gauthier also need to assume, or require, that risk-happy gamblers will not vote for an unequal system, hoping to be among the lucky ones who draw the cards of privilege.) That Veil of Ignorance, however, will never be opaque enough to secure its goal of impartiality, yet not so impenetrable as to conceal from me the very nature of my dispositions as the person I already am. Without any insight into the kind of person I am, however, there is little chance of my reliably assessing my likely response to all imaginable possibilities.

This point can be rephrased in familiar terms: Rawlsian Contractarianism is a kind of sophisticated version of the

Golden Rule, familiar to Christians from Luke 6:31 or Matthew 7:12: 'Do unto others as you would have them do unto you.' The Golden Rule fails if I don't share your tastes. But the diversity of tastes and preferences among cultures and among individuals is hard to exaggerate. Evidence for this is easy to find even if we restrict ourselves to very basic tastes in food and sex. On food, if you doubt this, I suggest you visit the Museum of Disgusting Foods in Malmö, Sweden. Any food offered for tasting is highly prized as a delicacy in some part of the world. But you will be provided with a sick bag, against your probable response to foods that will trigger extreme disgust. Much the same is true of sex: a few visits on dating apps should suffice to see that what some crave you find revolting, and that whatever you crave some would find disgusting.

If this applies to simple physical pleasures of food and sex, which natural selection might have been expected to allocate equally to every member of a species, it must a fortiori be true of the more complex preferences that result from individual temperament and socio-cultural conventions. In those, we can expect an unfathomable diversity. Where no general correspondence links situations to the experiences they elicit, the prospect of designing a set of universally applicable rules seems hopeless.

These considerations undermine the project of assessing and comparing the desirabilities of objective situations. Since such assessments are essential to computations of consequences for individual and collective happiness, they are highly relevant to the next approach to the question of ultimate justification.

3

Experience taught me that none of the things I feared contained in themselves anything either good or bad, except in the effect they had upon my mind.

Baruch de Spinoza (1632–1677)

The answers to the question of moral justification surveyed in the last chapter were all found either to be non-starters, too vague be clearly incompatible with amoralism or incapable of demarcating the moral domain in a way compatible with the aspiration to universality.

The first two sections of this chapter complement Chapter 2 by sketching two more approaches in broad outlines. These two approaches will figure in subsequent discussions. They are Utilitarian Consequentialism and Kantian Deontology. They are arguably currently the most influential ethical systems. I then introduce noncognitivist construals of moral language. These are ways of thinking about morality that differ from all the ones previously discussed in that they do not presuppose facts of morality independent of human attitudes. Noncognitive theories reinterpret the language of morality as expressing attitudes or emotions. They thereby bring us one step closer to amoralism.

UTILITARIAN CONSEQUENTIALISM

In the absence of a divine agent with the authority to issue commands, a common way of answering the 'Why should I do X?' question is to look to the likely consequences of X. If the consequences are likely to be good, do X; if not, refrain. But how are those consequences assessed?

Following John Stuart Mill (1803–1873), Utilitarianism answers our why-questions in terms of general happiness and unhappiness. Those, in turn, are evaluated on the basis of pleasures and pains (Mill, 1991[1861]).

Not everyone agrees that happiness can be assessed on that basis. Hedonism, the view that pleasure and pain are the ultimate criteria of happiness, can seem too narrow and superficial a basis for judging goodness and rightness; some insist that we should demand a wider understanding of happiness as 'eudaimonia', a richer concept of thriving or flourishing that values meaningful activity over pleasant experience. For now, however, we can grant that pleasure and pain are good candidates for the role of ultimate justifiers. If the answer to 'Why do X?' is 'Because it leads to or amounts to doing Y', you can follow up by asking what is desirable about Y. That starts a string of justifying reasons. But when Y consists in procuring pleasure, or relieving pain, to press a further question 'Why?' seems either uncomprehending or callous, unless there are compelling reasons to endure the pain or forgo the pleasure. In that sense, pain and pleasure are reliable *why-stoppers*.

Nevertheless, the Utilitarian answer gives rise to a host of problems. In addition to the question of the relation of pleasure and pain to happiness, we can ask: How reliable is our prediction of consequences? How far in the future should our calculations go? Who is the best judge of the goodness of a pleasure or the badness of a pain?

KANTIAN DEONTOLOGY

The word comes from the Greek to deon, meaning 'what ought to be' or 'what ought to be done'. 'Deontology' in general designates any kind of moral system that focuses on moral oughts. But it has come to be associated most closely with the philosopher Immanuel Kant (1724–1804), who held that a moral imperative or command, as distinct from any other kind of imperative or command, is 'categorical'—that is, unconditional and exceptionless (Kant, 1998 [1785]). It judges the morality of actions on the basis of their inherent character, independently of their consequences in any particular case.

Moral rules are typically contrasted with 'prudential' norms intended to promote self-interest. Prudential norms are merely 'hypothetical' or 'conditional'. They typically dictate what an agent 'should' do if they are pursuing some objective, as in 'If you want to cook an egg, start by opening the fridge'. A hypothetical imperative applies only as long as it does not conflict with some other more important goal. Kant argues that categorical imperatives, by contrast, yield to none other, because they derive from the essential nature of a rational agent. According to Kant, any intentional action involves acting for a reason, and an agent's capacity to act on a reason entails that such an agent is rational. Furthermore, it follows from the concept of rationality that any rational agent is committed to acting in the same way in the same situation.

Kant proposed a test to determine whether an act A is permissible: Could you envisage, without incoherence, a world in which it was a law of nature that anyone in the same situation did A? If not, the act is forbidden.

This rule has been ingeniously defended by Kant and his followers. From the point of view of common sense, however, it admits of only one example that is even moderately convincing. That example concerns lying. It works like this.

Suppose you are considering telling a lie. Kant urges you to ask whether you could coherently envisage a world in which the very laws of nature ensured that everyone always lied. It seems you could not, for in such a world, no one would believe anything they are told. And nothing really counts as a lie if there is no chance of anyone's being deceived by it. Lying is therefore absolutely forbidden. Kant goes as far as to insist that you may not lie even to protect the life of a friend fleeing from a pursuing murderer.

Note that if one rejects the demand for universalisation, the argument no longer works. If your policy is to lie only occasionally when you have a good chance of getting away with it, then it might be pointed out that there exists in fact just such a law of nature. It governs mimetism, a common occurrence in nature, by means of which one organism gains protection from predators by imitating the characteristic appearance of another organism or thing. The viceroy butterfly, for example, looks very like the poisonous monarch; so as long as both are around (the truth-telling monarchs as well as the lying viceroys), the deception can work, and the system endure.

There is a great deal more to the Kantian idea of the Categorical Imperative, including the suggestion that we look to a kind of ideal world. In that 'Kingdom of Ends', all regard every person as of absolute value in themself; no one values any person merely as a means to their own ends. It is hard to deny that such an ideal is an inspiring one. Yet one must also wonder whether it really makes sense to suppose that there is a single best way to be, both as an individual and as a member of a community. On the individual level, think of the vast ranges of preferences, aspirations, talents and possibilities exemplified across the world in time and space. Diversity is equally stunning in social arrangements. The sheer variety of social and political arrangements that have thrived on the face of the earth outstrips science fiction writers' imagination.

In rivalry with Utilitarianism, Kantian Deontology has gained allegiance from a great many philosophers. It too deserves more detailed consideration. It will become apparent that a principled reason for scepticism about morality derives from the impossibility of arriving at a reasonable principle of arbitration when faced with conflicts between the prescriptions derived from those two theories.

We shall look at both Utilitarianism and Kantian Deontology in more detail in Chapter 7. For now, let me introduce the radically different kind of answer that does not presuppose that there are objective facts—facts that exist regardless of our beliefs or attitudes—constituting the topic of morality.

NONCOGNITIVISM

The brief sketches I have so far provided of types of answers to why-questions illustrate two points. First, the problem of demarcating the moral domain is particularly stubborn given the clash between the insistence on universality and the cultural relativity of moral systems. Second, no single approach has proved sufficiently persuasive to produce consensus. What all share is the presupposition that moral imperatives stem from factual moral claims: they differ only in their explanations of the origin of those facts. In terms of the puzzle derived from Euthyphro's dilemma mentioned in the last chapter, the first six answers to the question of justification take the first branch: they answer the question 'Why should I regard something as right or good?' by attempting to provide objective criteria that will justify an agent's adoption of the value or the rule in question. All six of those answers are of the form 'We should adopt positive or negative attitudes to certain forms of behaviour *because they are right or good*'. By contrast, the thinkers considered in the present section—applying Euthyphro's dilemma to themselves rather than to Zeus—endorse the alternative branch. They maintain that some things are good or right *because they deem (or feel) them to be*. The present section explores the suggestion that morality does not consist in any normative moral truths that provide us with reasons to act. Instead, the converse is true: what appear to be objective prescriptions of morality are derived from subjective attitudes.

Internal and external

One feature of imperatives or prohibitions I have so far ignored is that they can be viewed from a point of view that is either internal or external to an agent. This duality of perspectives exists without regard to the objectivity of the entities or facts under debate. Most things in the universe, including—as we shall see in more detail in Chapter 5—the mechanisms of your own motivation, are and will forever remain unknown to you. When you become aware of some tiny sliver of that infinite set of facts, you may respond with some attitude, some emotion or some decision to act. In Divine Command Theory, for example, God's command is presumed to exist independently of the minds of those to whom it is addressed. Whether or not it seems compelling, whether it is welcome or resented, justified or arbitrary, heeding it presupposes that it comes from outside your own mind. You have to 'believe in it'.[1] As with commands, so with values: when you respond emotionally to some fact or situation you care about, it can seem as if that value would exist even if you failed to care. When you fear what is dangerous, are angered by what is offensive or are sad because of a loss, you are convinced that those conditions exist objectively and *merit* your response.

But what if that were just an illusion, much like the feeling, when you are in love, that your love can never die? What if the dangerous, the offensive, the sad or the good were not properties external to you, to which apt emotions respond, but mere projections of that very response onto the facts or situations that your emotions target? To fear a snarling dog, or to be sad about your cancelled date, feels as if it is justified by the fearsome quality of the dog, or the regrettable character of your prospects for the evening. But perhaps those value qualities, unlike the facts and laws studied by physics, have no existence independent of my attitude; perhaps there is no 'value property' in the dog, or in your date's change of plans. Those are just facts, devoid of intrinsic positive or negative value. In that case, the answer to the Euthyphro question would be the internalist or subjectivist one. The direction of fit of our responses' normative component would be world-to-mind. Any ought-statement would be relative to what a given agent *wants*, in the broad sense in which I am taking that word. The world of value would be constituted entirely by humans' emotional responses, actual or potential. There would be no essential difference between the origins of any moral value such as kindness or benevolence and an individual's purely subjective preference for a colour or flavour.

On that second tine of Euthyphro's fork, moral properties and more generally values, including good and bad, right and wrong, are merely projected onto the targets of emotions by those emotions themselves.

Those whose thinking runs along these lines are known as noncognitivists: for in their view there is nothing in the moral domain to be known.

Noncognitivism in one form or another has had many advocates in the history of philosophy. One early variant of this view was expressed by Baruch de Spinoza (1632–1677), as quoted in this chapter's epigraph. (Spinoza, 2020 [1677] 1.1). That was also, as we saw in Chapter 1, the view of David Hume. Hume wrote: 'When I am angry, I am actually possest with the passion, and in that emotion have no more a reference to any other object, than when I am thirsty, or sick, or more than five foot high' (Hume, 1978 [1739], 2.3.3.5). We are accustomed to thinking that 'beauty is in the eye of the beholder', and if we burn our finger on a flame, we find it natural to think the heat is in the flame; the pain, by contrast, is only in my finger, or more precisely in my experience of the state of my finger. According to emotionists, the same is true of the fearful, the sad, the offensive and the morally good or evil. Values, ought-statements and imperatives exist only insofar as the items that seem to instantiate them are met with a certain emotional attitude. That attitude is then trivially viewed as appropriate to its target.

More recent variants of Noncognitivism have seized on the fact that not all uses of language are meant to do what their syntax suggests. 'How are you?' and 'How do you do?' are not really questions; 'You know' is not really a statement. The Logical Positivist philosopher A. J. Ayer (1910–1989) followed Hume in arguing that an ought or value judgment is not a proposition that could be true or false, even when it seems to be. Instead, it simply amounts to an expression of approval or disapproval, roughly equivalent to 'Booh!' or 'Hurrah' (Ayer, 1936). Later, the American philosopher Charles Stevenson (1908–1979) argued that moral judgments are expressions of personal attitudes or emotions that are intended to be persuasive. He argued that in addition to being expressions of attitudes of approval or disapproval, moral utterances carry an implicit prescription for others to adopt the same attitudes (Stevenson, 1944). And R. M. Hare (1919–2002) melded that idea of prescriptivism with the traditional moralist's requirement for universalisability. On his view, moral judgments are universalisable and have the form of imperative statements. For example, when someone says, 'You ought to tell the truth', they are neither making a statement of fact nor expressing a personal preference. Rather, they are prescribing a universal principle of behaviour. They are saying, in effect, 'Everyone! Always tell the truth!' (Hare, 1952).

Whether moral statements are understood as expressions of approval or disapproval, or of emotions, or as prescriptions or commands, each member of this family of views denies the existence of any moral facts. Despite their differences, they can all be regarded as holding variants of 'Projectivism', a general term for the second prong of Euthyphro's fork. For Projectivism, values and moral commands are not apprehensions of an objective reality in the moral domain, but simply projections of affective responses—typically taking the form of emotional attitudes—to facts or situations in the world (D'Arms & Jacobson, 2007).

It is important to note that moral utterances may still face demands for justification, even for a noncognitivist.

Whether you are saying 'Booh' or 'Hurray', expressing an emotion or uttering a prescription, particularly if you are claiming some sort of authority in doing so which extends to everybody, you can be challenged to provide a justifying explanation. Even when we say, 'I don't know why I feel this way', we are recognising a need to justify the feeling. Often we just make up an answer, whether or not anyone else finds it plausible.

Projectivism as provocation

Here, then, is the upshot so far of our brief tour of ultimate answers to why-questions. Whether we interpret moral statements as making objective claims about the world outside us, or see them merely as projections of our emotional responses to facts, we need to explain how utterances can be justified. A justification can be found more or less compelling. But the least it must do is to be accepted as a why-stopper.

To conclude that there is nothing more to moral rightness or moral good than a projection of purely subjective feeling will strike many as little more than a provocation—an intellectual scandal. That sense of scandal helped to motivate the rejection of the simplistic 'booh-hurrah' version advocated by A. J. Ayer in favour of the more sophisticated versions of Noncognitivism elaborated by Stevenson and Hare. One way to mitigate the counterintuitive character of Noncognitivism regarding normative claims is to insist that it is compatible with a certain kind of reconstructed realism about values. For despite their subjective character, value statements express— even if they do not assert—facts about our *dispositions to care*. Rather than a source of mere illusion, the facts about what matters to people constitute the raw material of a kind of value that has as much objective reality as can be reasonably wished for. What we think of as values, as opposed to mere subjective preferences, are created or constructed on the basis of those individual preferences, approvals and disapprovals. The process of that construction involves other members of our community, forming a network of mutual validation, articulation and criticism that ultimately results in an evolving collective moral understanding; yet according to Projectivism, there is no reality to those 'values' beyond the individual preferences that go into their construction.

I will return to the question of how some measure of objectivity might be constructed out of a convergence of subjective attitudes. But for the moment I want to set aside any mitigating refinements. Rather than trying to amend Projectivism, conceived as the view that values are simply projections of our emotional responses, I want to show how even a radical subjectivism about values, goodness or right and wrong might seem plausible and even banal once we look at it from a different perspective.

The biological ubiquity of feeling: detection and response

The crucial step in this reframing of our conception of value is to realise that nothing can *matter* unless it matters *to* some conscious being. It must matter specifically to one whose consciousness is capable of *caring*. The notion of caring involved here is minimal: caring can be either positive or negative. When positive, it looks for the promotion or continuation of some state; it is negative when it seeks its removal or avoidance. Understood thus, we could think of a bacterium as caring. That would merely require us to surmise that a capacity for sentience, or *feeling*, complements the bacterium's capacities of detection and response. The bacterium's feelings would consist in a conscious awareness of the tropisms that cause its approach or avoidance responses. That would imply that there is a characteristic 'what it's like' to detection leading to approach, and another to detection leading to avoidance. To be sure, we have independent reasons for denying that bacteria have feelings. As far as we know. you need a brain to be sentient,[2] and bacteria have no brains. But beside that, what is it about sentience that makes some things matter?

The answer, I suggest, is that without sentience the very idea of something's mattering makes no sense. Although we are apt to describe something as mattering or not mattering without qualification, the unqualified phrase is understood as taking for granted that there is some sentient being (especially you or your friends) who might care. If something matters, it must matter to some sentient being.

That does not, however, establish the reciprocal: it does not show that if something matters to me, then it matters, period. Projectivism appears to countenance the possibility that something might matter *only to me*. But if something matters just to me, could that be enough to make it matter without qualification? You might be inclined to think that what is purely subjective can't objectively matter—that what matters *only* to you doesn't *really* matter. And if mattering-to-you is the only way anything matters, then nothing *really* matters.

And if nothing really matters, wouldn't that be awful?

Well, no, I say. To be awful is to matter; if nothing mattered, nothing could be awful. If you think it would be *really* awful if nothing mattered, take comfort: you have just manifested your conviction that something *really* matters after all.

If you think that your own caring cannot make anything significant, it may be that you feel one of two further conditions must be met for something to be significant: either to have been justified or endorsed by an external authority whose decrees are unquestionable, or to be grounded in some reality that exists independently of what you care about. How can we assess these two conditions?

The only direct way to meet the first condition is to return to Divine Command Theory, and declare your allegiance to whatever God commands. The provocation is dismissed, the scandal is avoided: things matter, and would continue to matter even if there were no sentient beings, because they matter to God.[3] But I shall regard as conclusive the reasons already alluded to for rejecting that option.

Justifying emotional responses

What of the second condition: can it be met by Projectivism? Can emotions be justified by some reality independent of any sentient being's attitudes?

The short answer is that emotions can indeed be justified or unjustified. You have no reason to be angry at me if I have not done something to harm you; you have good reason to grieve if you have lost a loved one. But notice that those examples have no need to posit any value or 'normative fact'. Each needs to appeal only to properties intelligible as *reasons* for the emotion in question. Such properties can be ordinary, factual, non-normative ones. Call them *natural* properties. A justifying natural property just has to be one that the agent cares about in the right way—that is, in a way that makes it a reason to feel or to act.

As I use the expression, natural properties to which respond emotionally may originate in social or institutional conventions. Legal facts like those of marriage or property, for example, have their own normative implications for anyone who participates in those institutions or conventions. I include them in the class of natural facts or properties. For even social facts created by human-made institutions are objective from the point of view of any particular individual. Their objective character subsists even for an individual who may not agree that they should have been created in the first place.[4]

The domain of what we care about is the domain of emotions. It is not surprising that many thinkers have concluded that the ultimate explanations for the way we conduct ourselves, and for the way in which we attempt to justify our conduct, lie in our nature as beings capable of experiencing emotions. This calls for some further elaboration.

Emotions and morality

Psychologists and philosophers have constructed competing theories of emotion. While there remains much debate, a few generalities command widespread assent. We can characterise emotion informally as a kind of feeling, directed at a target situation, person or thing, which typically motivates a behavioural response. However complex human emotions may have become, their basic function involves capacities that were essential for the continued maintenance of the most primitive forms of life. As already noted, even a unicellular organism—of the sort that still accounts for by far the greatest number of living things on earth—must be equipped with the capacity to *detect* and *respond*.

Despite the fantasies indulged a few pages back, the exercise of these capacities requires no sentience. They are simply mechanisms, no more mysterious than James Watts's engine governor, the spinning arms of which keep an engine's speed within a range of desirable values by opening or closing a throttle. Two basic responses, approach and avoidance, are the most primitive forms of positive and negative *valence*.

In philosophy or psychology, the term *valence* functions as a very general way to capture the polarities of pleasure and displeasure, satisfaction and dissatisfaction, or generic good and bad. It is an intentionally vague term which covers types of evaluation that are only distantly related, without distinction among the ways we can regard something positively or negatively: pleasant and unpleasant; useful and harmful; admirable and contemptible; virtuous and vicious; beautiful and ugly. And, most general of all, good and bad—in a sense that does nothing to help us identify what might be special about morality.

With some exceptions, we are generally confident in identifying the valence of a given emotion as positive or negative. Fear is negative; admiration is positive; disgust is negative, joy positive; disappointment is negative, amusement positive; anxiety is negative, contentment positive.

Notice two complications. First, emotions are typically consciously experienced. Second, most of our emotions are essentially social: their targets usually are or involve other people.

The first implies that not only are emotions valenced responses to something in the world, but they are also in themselves experienced as pleasant or unpleasant. Some irascible people, for example, enjoy being angry. As a response to some thing or event, their anger's valence remains negative, but the subjective experience of anger may be positive.

Conversely, erotic desire surely attributes a positive valence to its target, but in itself it can be acutely painful.

Second, the social character of emotions also entails that their expression itself elicits further emotional responses from their targets. It is pleasant to be the recipient of an expression of gratitude. It is unpleasant to be the target of anger. A typical emotional scenario might then involve valence on three levels: that of the emotion itself considered as a response to its target, that of the emoter's experience as pleasant or unpleasant, and that of the further response elicited from the person targeted by the original emotion.

About some emotions, we may feel ambivalent. Pride, for example, has a positive valence from the point of view of the subject who experiences pride, but it is sometimes the object of disapproval. So we can infer, at least, from the fact that pride is listed as one of the seven deadly sins in Christian theology. That negative evaluation is made from a point of view outside that of the agent, but it can affect the agent's own experience in so far as they have internalised that disapproval. In some contexts, however, such as 'a proud parent' or 'take pride in your work', pride elicits approval and has positive valence for both subject and observer.

Once we identify a given emotion, we also usually have an idea of the kind of behaviour it might motivate. Emotions are the distant inheritor of our unicellular ancestors' capacities for detection and response.

As our forebears evolved into increasingly complex animals, they acquired conscious memory, foresight and an increasingly sophisticated capacity to construct an inner model of their 'niche'—their environment as it affects them. As a result, the mere detection of a stimulus has come to involve an elaborate network of sense organs, the inputs of which are used to construct a representation of an increasingly complex world.

Many features of that world remain unavailable to other mammals lacking human language. Together with other tools, language enhances our sensory organs and behavioural possibilities. We can now manipulate elementary particles, or probe the beginning of our universe. This has enabled the construction of new and potentially unlimited models of the world far beyond our biological niche. To take advantage of these resources, our brains needed to develop capacities for abstraction and inference. As technology keeps enlarging the range of what we can detect and respond to, our domain now reflects ever greater varieties of relationships, expectations and sources of pleasure and pain. All these are now inherent in the social world we have constructed.

Still, for all that is radically new and would have been unimaginable a million years ago, our emotions retain, in common with our earliest multicellular ancestors, the basic dual functions of detecting and responding. They determine what we care about. That is why we are so often willing to kill or to die for the sake of our 'values', modified and refined as they have been both by biological and by cultural evolution, or 'gene-culture co-evolution' working in inextricable collaboration. (See Box #2 in Chapter 12.)

As we have seen, evolution cannot be expected consistently to do things for the best. Neither can culture, as is plainly attested by the crimes and human-made catastrophes facilitated by public enthusiasm. The emotions, motivations and behavioural tendencies brought about by gene-culture co-evolution would be far from being universally endorsed even if they were consistent. For most of us, the principles of conduct to which we are inclined to subscribe are simply borrowed from those that prevail around us. We tend to ignore the fact that what people regard as morally important and correct differs from one time and place to another. To justify your endorsement, you would have to embark on a process of justification that would ineluctably drag you into an endless morass of philosophical dispute—as I shall illustrate in Chapter 7.

The threat of trivial self-justification

In the absence of any standard outside my own mind for what is worth valuing, it might appear that deliberation would be pointless. If a want suffices to make its object good, my every want is trivially self-justifying. That seems to imply that Projectivism can make no distinction between your horror of slavery, torture or monstrous injustice and your preference for vanilla over chocolate ice cream. But surely, you will say, that is preposterous. Your horror of slavery is justified by its objective inherent evil, while your taste in ice cream is purely subjective. Injustice would still be horrible if you felt no horror. Indeed, such indifference should be regarded as a disability. Like colour-blindness that makes it impossible to tell two paint chips of different hues apart, it would constitute an impairment of your capacity to see the world as it is.

These objectivist intuitions are powerful. But several responses are available to the projectivist. One of these takes up the case of colour as an analogy.

Light waves of different frequencies are perceived as different colours, and the combination of light frequencies reaching the retina depends on their proximate source, such as the micro-structure of the surface reflecting them. But there is no one-to-one correspondence between an experience of hue and some given light frequency. Our colour sensations result from combinations of the ratios between the responses of different types of retinal cone cells to a given set of light frequencies. Several different combinations of light frequencies might yield indistinguishable colour sensations under otherwise identical conditions. Hence, given the complexity of the ways in which a surface's micro-texture can result in our seeing it as mauve, there is no one set of conditions, in the micro-structure of a reflective surface and background lighting, that is necessary and sufficient to trigger the sensation of a given shade of mauve. Nevertheless, we could simply define the property 'mauve' as the disjunction of all the conditions that possess the power to produce a sensation of 'mauve' in normal viewers. The definition would be correct regardless of our ignorance about the actual electromagnetic properties of each member of that disjunctive set.

Similarly, we might find it difficult if not impossible to specify the natural properties of situations that persons respond to with an attitude of fear. But we could simply define the property of the *fearsome* as the disjunctive set of conditions, any of which is sufficient to trigger fear in persons exposed to the situation in question. The quality of being fearsome would then simply be whatever it takes for something to trigger fear.

Philosophers have not ignored this analogy with colour. But they have pointed out that it does not actually achieve what would satisfy those who are scandalised by Projectivism. For the property thus defined (let us stay with the *fearsome*), while objective, is also non-normative. If a situation has the property *fearsome*, as defined, then it does not justify my fear: it merely causes it. What is missing is not a mere specification of a natural property, however complex, but an explanation of why some properties *justify* or even *require* the emotional attitude of fear. Or, to put it differently, how some complex natural properties appear to constitute or give rise to a norm. What is 'normative' here, however, has nothing to do with morality or even any other kind of value; it merely refers to the conventions that govern the use of language, which dictate that 'fear' is apt only if the emotion it refers to targets something dangerous.

To explain how such conventions come about, we may surmise, would be to describe the process of calibration by which members of a given community attain a high degree of consensus on what to regard as a 'normal range' of responses expected in specific situation types. Such an explanation is needed, since even the most committed projectivist will recognise that there is a difference between something that is generally taken as a value, on one side, and a merely idiosyncratic response, on the other. The existence of such local consensus is a sociological fact resulting from a complicated network of causes.

Where emotions relate to 'moral' emotions and the values they correspond to, a full understanding of these causes would come from evolutionary theory, anthropology, history, sociology and psychology. The resulting explanation will describe why norms gain acceptance, how they function to guide or restrict behaviour and why they, like religious dogmas, not infrequently give rise to murderous quarrels. But such explanations will not, in themselves, provide any reason to accept any of the strictures, commands or prohibitions they describe. On the contrary, an understanding of the origins of moral convictions is likely to debunk them. Just as a thorough and sympathetic instruction in many religions is liable to inculcate religious scepticism (Dennett, 2006), so likewise a comprehensive explanation of the nature, origin and power of moral emotions might well convince a rational observer that their own morality lacks any objective justification and is best ignored.

What to conclude about Noncognitivism

Given the lack of consensus on the questions moralists consider important, the sketches of some strategies of justification in this and the previous chapter look discouraging. The sheer number of those strategies, and the fact that each one is subject to what often seem to be fatal objections; the absence of a more authoritative level of discourse that might decide between them—all that, I shall be arguing, makes the attempt to find the right moral system hopelessly quixotic. Like Don Quixote himself, philosophers have been as ingenious in their inventions as they have been diligent in their quest for the unattainable, universally valid algorithm that answers every practical question. In doing so, as I shall be arguing in more detail in Chapter 7, they have reached no consensus on when a situation needs to be considered from a moral point of view, on what reasons count as moral, or on the sources of the moral values they want to promote. They happily draw intuitions from thin air, devote whole careers to insoluble debates, and affect certainty about dogmas that encourage many of our most deplorable tendencies: self-righteous contempt, blame and guilt. I will suggest that we need not waste intellectual energy on attempts to demarcate 'moral' from all other concerns. We have much to gain and little to lose by attending directly and more equitably to the variety of our *reasons* for acting, believing and feeling. As I shall argue in more detail in Chapters 5 and 6, our reasons can be sufficiently grounded in our beliefs about how the world is, together with what we care about and want.

The purpose of this chapter has been to sketch the two most influential answers on offer to the question of justification of morality, and to present a radically noncognitivist or projectivist alternative. To be sure, the mere existence of a wide variety of incompatible views does not prove that none is objectively correct. It would therefore be premature to claim that the quest for an answer must have been deluded in the first place. Nevertheless, the argument so far suggests that in the absence of good reasons to accept the existence of objective facts of normative morality, a noncognitivist account of the nature of moral convictions as projections of our emotional responses is defensible. That account begins by denying the existence of any moral facts, and provides no reason to reject the kind of moral relativism that is illustrated by conflicting cultural norms. Since relativism is a position that most moralists regard as incoherent, its acceptance would create a strong prima facie case in favour of amoralism.

In what follows, I shall focus on a number of other problems that may tend to favour abolitionism. I begin, in the next chapter, by illustrating the tendency of the main ethical theories to become totalising in repugnant ways.

Moral systems tend to be totalising

4

In England, everything is permitted, except what is forbidden.
In Germany, everything is forbidden, except what is permitted.
In France, everything is permitted, even what is forbidden.
In Russia, everything is forbidden, even what is permitted.

Attributed to Winston Churchill (1874–1965)

Christians are told in Luke 12:7 that 'the very hairs on your head are all counted'. God sees your every act and knows your every thought. To be the object of such a fine-grained attention from the Omnipotent (the very hairs on my head!), while it may be comforting to some ('God loves ME!'), feels creepy to others. Or even terrifying, if you remember that Adam and Eve, in their innocence, were condemned to endless generations of suffering for a pecadillo. Their crime: choosing to acquire the very knowledge of right and wrong that presumably would be required to tell that disobedience would be wrong. God does not merely see: *He judges*.

Principles of conduct are typically embodied in the teachings of religions. Some are precepts designed to promote community among adherents; others consist in rules that philosophers would recognise as 'moral principles'. Examples of the former are the injunction not to 'take the Lord's name in vain', to avoid worshipping 'graven images', or to undertake the Hajj. Alms, truth-telling, respect for life and property

DOI: 10.4324/9781003278252-4

illustrate the latter. Theologians elaborate on the first sort. Moral philosophers strive to demarcate the latter domain and detail the commandments' application to practical life. But if we think of principles of conduct as recommendations or rules that govern specific acts or circumstances, it is natural to assume that not everything we think and do will either be demanded or forbidden. A life in which nothing is left to individual whim seems too depressing to endure.

Since four of the ten Judeo-Christian commandments are merely about stroking the Divine Ego, we might expect that a secular morality, even if it incorporates the other six, would leave greater scope for individual choice. Curiously, however, the opposite seems to be the case. The range of options left to individual choice and regarded as morally indifferent becomes surprisingly narrow when these options are assessed in the light of the principles developed by moral philosophers. Taken to their logical conclusions, the precepts dictated by some secular systems of morality appear to be hardly less stringent or invasive than the Taliban's. That is notably the case when chains of justification take the forms given to them by the widely followed schools of thought surveyed in the last two chapters. In addition, the problem of demarcation—how to tell imperatives in the moral domain from ones outside it—remains a pressing one that undermines the prospect of a moral consensus.

DEMARCATING MORALITY AGAIN

One approach to the demarcation problem begins by distinguishing three kinds of principles of conduct. One concerns religious obligations grounded in divine authority. A second comprises strategies for managing decisions aiming at an agent's own satisfaction. This is 'prudence', which contrasts with morality in that it offers only counsels of efficiency. From the point of view of prudence, both the goals and the means to attain them are considered without reference to morality. Economists and philosophers have systematised the deliberative processes of prudence as 'rational decision theory', aiming at maximising 'expected utility' (see Box #3). The third class of principles is the one crisply identified by Bernard Gert's definition of morality discussed in Chapter 1; it pertains to 'behavior that affects others . . . and has the lessening of evil or harm as its goal' (Gert, 2005, p. 14).

Gert's characterisation of the moral domain also implicitly defines a complementary category of the morally indifferent. If morality is about what affects others, then anything I do that does not affect others will be free of any moral constraints. Insofar as morality's goal is to minimise evil or harm, it will not be concerned with anything you do, providing it results in no harm. Your preference for vanilla ice over chocolate, for example, seems an obvious example. It affects no one else and is surely a harmless choice if anything is.

If *anything* is: the reservation is not trivial. Is anything really sure to affect no one else? And is anything really sure of being harmless?

There are three reasons to doubt this. One stems from the impossibility of insulating what we do from unintended meanings and unpredictable consequences. A second comes from the cultural dependency of ordinary people's conception of the moral domain. And a third comes from the nature of the very efforts philosophers have made to refine and systematise the principles that ground specific rules of moral conduct. The bulk of this chapter will be devoted to the third of these considerations. But first, let me briefly comment on the first two.

BOX #3 EXPECTED UTILITY

Expected utility (EU) is a measure that allows for the evaluation and comparison of actions. It is based on the desirability of each possible outcome, weighted by its probability.

EU is calculated by assigning a numerical value or 'utility' as well as a probability to each possible outcome of a decision. The utility of each is multiplied ('weighted') by its probability, and the results are added together to yield the expected value or utility of the act envisaged.

Example: It might rain. Should I take an umbrella?

There are two options, with four possible outcomes. The four steps to my decision are:

1. *Assign a utility value* to each possible outcome of the decision. E.g., **If rain**: getting wet = 1; staying dry = 10; **if no rain**: no umbrella = 15; carrying umbrella = 4.
2. *Assess the probabilities*: E.g., chance of rain = .7; no rain = .3.
3. *Calculate EU*: Multiply each outcome's utility by its corresponding probability and add them, as in the table below:

	RAIN (Prob= .7)	NO RAIN (Prob = .3)	EU CALCULATION	EXPECTED UTILITY
UMBRELLA	10	4	10 x .7 + 4 x .3 =	8.2
NO UMBRELLA	1	15	1 x .7 + 15 x .3 =	5.2

4. *The decision*: Compare the expected utilities of the different options. In this case, the expected utility of bringing an umbrella is higher than not bringing one. Bringing an umbrella is the better decision.

In general, for outcomes 1-i of decision D where p is the probability and v is the value of each outcome, the expected utility (EU) of D is expressed as:

$$EU(D) = \Sigma_{1\text{-}i} \, (p_i \times v_i)$$

Unintended meanings, unpredictable consequences

A moment's consideration suggests that even your choice of ice cream fails to be insulated from moral significance. If you google *vanilla*, you will find that 'the rising demand for vanilla poses several social and environmental concerns, including cases of child labour, deforestation, and the exploitation of farmers'. Its cultivation has led to major deforestation in the producing regions, notably Madagascar, affecting wildlife including '107 species of lemurs . . . found nowhere else on Earth', most of which are 'critically endangered' or 'threatened'.[1] Search for *chocolate* or *cocoa*, and you will see a similar story. Again, cacao cultivation involves deforestation and habitat destruction affecting elephants, chimpanzees and many other species, as well as child and slave labour.[2] Since a preference for one flavour of ice cream tends to be the first example that springs to mind of something morally indifferent, we should indeed doubt whether anything is. You should be feeling guilty even for lying in bed doing nothing, since there is surely something you *could* be doing to increase total happiness.

The cultural relativity of demarcation

The second reason for doubt derives from well-supported findings in social science. These show that among different cultures we find not only divergences of opinion about what is morally good and bad, but radically different assumptions about what counts as morally important.

Attempts have been made to find a universal intuition that differentiates moral from merely conventional prohibitions. Influential research by Elliot Turiel appeared to show that even young children can make the distinction. His way of operationalising this was simple but ingenious: he told his child subjects about a school where teachers said it was permissible to do *A* (e.g., (a) hit other children, or (b) wear unconventional clothes), and asked whether the teacher's approval made *A* permissible. The children judged that if teachers said doing *A* was all right, that would make *A* permissible in some cases like (b), but it would still be wrong in cases like (a)—thus correctly differentiating, Turiel claimed, merely conventional from genuinely moral prohibitions (Turiel, 1983).

Critics pointed out that moral transgressions are generally regarded as far more serious than mere failures of etiquette. It is therefore difficult to gauge the extent to which the children's judgments simply reflected the heavier stress laid by their parents or teachers on some kinds of prohibitions over others.

Furthermore, while norms inculcated in early childhood include both moral and conventional rules, the line between them varies. Social science has distinguished different areas or domains that morality is concerned with, but the relative importance of those domains varies in major ways from one social group to another. Two of these domains correspond closely to Gert's definition: they are *avoidance of harm* and *promotion of fairness* or *reciprocity*. The others are grouped somewhat differently by different scholars, but the clearest classification, due to Jonathan Haidt, comprises *purity/sanctity*, *ingroup/loyalty*, and *authority/respect* (Haidt & Joseph, 2007). Others identify the first with *divinity*, and merge the latter two into *community* (Shweder, Much, Mahapatra, & Park, 2000). While the avoidance of harm and a concern for fairness are generally regarded as central to morality in modern liberal or WEIRD societies, the three others are accorded comparable or even greater importance in more conservative societies or subcultures. If what counts as morality differs in important ways among cultural groups, we must expect conflicts between considerations of harm avoidance or fairness on the one hand and the bonds of loyalty, hierarchy or religion on the other.

Consider, for example, a business CEO who is an immigrant to a modern Western country from a non-WEIRD one in which kinship ties are paramount. When making a hiring decision, such a person might experience the need to balance considerations of fairness and merit against cultural expectations of family loyalty. If the CEO hires an outsider over an inept cousin in need of a job, their family may experience the decision as a betrayal of their moral duty to their kin. To the CEO's Western colleagues, on the contrary, that decision seems required on the basis of fairness as well as efficiency, while the 'duty' of loyalty to kin is morally unacceptable nepotism.

We must conclude that in Gert's definition the avoidance of harm clashes with the demand for universality. If what counts as harm differs widely from one time, place or culture to another, then the moralist must renounce the claim to universality and accept some form of moral relativism. Otherwise, the moralist owes us, if not a conclusive defence of their specific moral theory, at least a method for constructing a theory that everyone can accept. A successful theory would pave the way for a clear line of demarcation between the moral and the non-moral, as well as generating reliably universalisable rules of conduct. I shall confront the clash of titans attempting to meet this challenge in Chapter 7.

The totalising character of moral theories

I come now to the third reason to regard morality as excessively invasive. I do this by sketching how, in the two most widely followed philosophical elaborations of moral theory, the principles of morality extend their tentacles to virtually every choice. Two specific examples admittedly don't show that every possible theory must follow suit, but they can serve as illustrations of a tendency and a challenge to alternative theories.

My two illustrative examples are Utilitarian and Kantian theories. Just as, in Christian theology, venial sins can be forgiven while still being regarded as sins, so the champions of those theories will exempt some acts from moral blame in practice. But this will not be because the theories exonerate them. It will merely be due to an arbitrary threshold of importance. They simply benefit from ad hoc intellectual acrobatics, by means of which moral systems insulate themselves from their own more repugnant implications.

In this respect, morality contrasts instructively with law. In law, many things are forbidden, and many are required. But law leaves much to individual choice that is neither compulsory nor forbidden. Over the last couple of centuries, although laws and regulations have proliferated, and antiquated ones often remain on the books even when not enforced, legislation in advanced countries has tended to extend the domain of individual freedoms.

That trend, we can hope, will persist despite the alarming signs of regression that we have recently witnessed in the United States and elsewhere. These regressive steps, which are invariably backed by moralistic or religious convictions that have little to do with fairness or harm prevention, have been dire. We have witnessed the withdrawal of protections against racial discrimination and voter suppression; the proscription from education and research of uncomfortable facts and enduring consequences of slavery; the banning of books; and the usurpation by unqualified judges or politicians of health care decisions best left to individuals and their medical caretakers. All of these have worked to abridge individual freedom (often, in an Orwellian twist, in the name of freedom).

Nevertheless, the general tendency over the past century has been to broaden the range of decisions that are left to individual preference. In modern pluralistic societies, it has come to be widely agreed that the law should not enforce every moral norm. Accordingly, modern law has increasingly designated certain areas of life as falling in the 'private' sphere. Legislators have withdrawn from regulating that sphere even when a vocal minority continue to regard some behaviours as 'immoral'. Sex and religion provide obvious examples. Blasphemy laws are seldom enforced even where they are not repealed. And most now agree with Pierre Trudeau, then Minister of Justice and later Prime Minister of Canada, who decreed in 1967 that 'the State has no place in the bedrooms of the nation'.

In short, the trend to greater legal autonomy has reduced the law's subservience to traditional conceptions of morality. But moralists have resisted and are still attempting to reverse our liberation from its intrusive meddling. Far from shrinking, the domain morality aspires to regulate includes many new things for us to blame or feel guilty about, even when the law remains permissive. The intuitions that ordinary people have about what counts as moral behaviour have changed in many parts of the world. But while some prohibitions have softened, many others seem to have come to replace them.

While adult consensual sex, in its rainbow diversity, has in most WEIRD subcultures ceased to be a target of harrumphing moralists, some areas that were previously regarded as outside the moral purview seem to have replaced it. The psychologist Steven Pinker has even suggested that a 'law of conservation of moralising' ensures that as we remove some items from the list of immoral behaviours, others take their place. He notes that in liberal circles homosexuality, divorce and marijuana are now off the list, but eating meat, driving SUVs and smoking tobacco have replaced them (Pinker, 2008).

What that suggests is that the psychological tendency to moralise—to regard others and even oneself as worthy of blame or punishment—is easily triggered. In itself, that is no more than a psychological observation. Remarkably, however, it seems not to be limited to morality as it is popularly conceived. From the most influential systems of morality constructed by philosophers, it seems that pretty much anything we do is either morally good or morally bad. (And while any one action may be good in some respects and bad in others, there are always more ways of being bad than good.) Moralists recognise the *permitted*, of course, but that raises the same unanswerable question: who issued the permission? It too lies in the moral domain, which the moral abolitionist rejects.

The imperialism of morality seems to hold equally for Utilitarianism and for Kantian Deontology. Both implicitly or explicitly discard Gert's restriction to 'behavior that affects others'. In Utilitarianism, as we have seen, the Principle of Utility demands that we assess any prospective decision in terms of its likely effects on 'the total happiness of the greatest number'. Since you are included in that number, even what concerns only you affects the total, and so cannot strictly be morally insignificant. Similarly, Kantian Deontology requires you to test any thought or deed against the 'Categorical Imperative', which is supposed to follow from the mere fact that you are a rational agent. In practice, both these theories of morality will mitigate their overreach by declaring some actions morally neutral, but they can do so, I shall argue, only by setting arbitrary limits to their own relevance.

I begin with Utilitarianism.

MAXIMISING UTILITY

As defined by John Stuart Mill's classic exposition, the Principle of Utility sets the happiness of the greatest number as the ultimate measure of value (Mill, 1991 [1861]). Mill's account, as we saw, is hedonist, while others prefer to speak of a wider conception invoking eudaimonia. In either version, the theory involves the sum of 'utils' provided by pleasure or other positive experiences minus the sum of pain or displeasure contained in each human life.[3] Whether hedonistic or eudaimonistic, Utilitarianism needs to pin down just what count as utils and how they are to be measured and compared. Mill, for example, struggled to make an intelligible distinction between the quantity or intensity of a pleasure and its quality. He argued that 'higher' pleasures, typically those taken in intellectual or aesthetic experience, are generally preferable to 'lower' or merely physical pleasures of the sort typically afforded by bodily sensations, even when the latter are more intense or their attraction more immediate.

For Eudaimonistic utilitarians, happiness is tied to a more holistic conception of the 'good life', dependent more on the satisfaction derived from meaningful activity, variety of experience, human connection and the completion of projects. Eudaimonia is the kind of thing Virtue Theories prize, as the well-being that results from the fulfilment of the potential in one's idiosyncratic nature. It is therefore particularly difficult to measure. Indeed, according to Aristotle himself, your eudaimonia cannot properly be assessed until after you are dead, and maybe not even then. (Utilitarians generally don't go quite that far.) However hard it might be to measure the sum of an individual's trove of pleasures and pains, therefore, the happiness of a life in terms of 'eudaimonia' is incalculably more difficult. And since every life necessarily has proliferating effects on many others, total happiness can be no more determinate than its parts.

Consider, to take just two classic examples, how one might appraise the Homeric hero Achilles' choice of a short but glorious life over a long and cheerful but uneventful one, or compare a life devoted to saintly or heroic virtue with that of a genius whose commitment to artistic achievement or scientific knowledge bequeathed us a timeless masterpiece or profound discovery. In every case of this kind, the choice's consequences for the total happiness of its protagonist constitute only a tiny portion of its relevant effects on the 'happiness of the greatest number'.

Whatever turns out to be the most appropriate interpretation of the happiness to be maximised, the theory cannot dispense with measurable 'utils'. Assuming that there is a solution to the problem of converting experiences into utils, however, I want now to stress that Utilitarianism should commit us to regarding our every choice as morally significant.

Butterfly effects

That idea was already adumbrated a few pages back, in connection with the dire if distant harms resulting from apparently trivial choices. Even the most apparently innocent action is at the point of convergence of myriad causes and myriad effects. The conditions that motivate any particular action have resulted from a long chain of events that an omniscient being could track 14 billion years back to the Big Bang—with or without a sprinkling of purely random turns. In its consequences, an agent's every decision, like even the smallest pebble dropped into a still lake, originates a cascade of crisscrossing ripples. The substitution of a molecule in a strand of DNA must have been one cause, after a few million years and a few more such substitutions, of the existence of the human species. What appears unimportant at the time of its occurrence might always have unpredicted consequences of great moment. That is the lesson of the notorious 'butterfly effect' aspect of chaotic systems.[4]

It used to seem obvious that a simple and apparently insignificant cause could never have momentous effects. Theologians inferred from this that only a cause even greater and more complex than the Universe could account for what exists—that cause being an all-powerful Creator. The butterfly effect refutes that assumption. As does the fact that a tiny random cause, such as the accidental substitution of a molecule in a strand of DNA, has resulted in the existence of our species.

It seems reasonable to conclude that nothing in the logic of Consequentialism or of Utilitarianism can exempt any act or thought, on principle, from being fed into the voracious Calculator of Overall Utility. The desirability of performing or refraining from any act should ideally be computed from the value of every one of its possible consequences. But what are those? None is certain. So every possible consequence must be weighted by its probability, which is itself, in most cases, no more than subjective surmise.

Rules of thumb

When confronting the practical impossibility of the task just described, some utilitarians introduce a variant form of Consequentialism referred to as Rule Consequentialism or Rule Utilitarianism (*Hooker, 2023). That variant modifies the original invitation to assess the predictable consequences of each option before deciding how to act, known as Act Consequentialism. The idea of Rule Utilitarianism is that even if we grant that the consequences of any particular action can never be determined—at least beyond what seems immediately obvious but may well be undone shortly after—we can make reasonable estimates of statistical probabilities, applicable to types of actions rather than particular acts. Providing we are optimistic about our capacity to draw reliable lessons from history and sociology, it seems likely that a community will fare better when its members reliably act with honesty, compassion and kindness, and refrain from selfishness and cruelty. Since many act types will fail to produce consistently good or consistently bad results simply when considered in themselves, we could designate those as forming a class of acts that are neither required nor forbidden, thus escaping the totalising tendency of morality.

That ploy, however, really amounts to a retreat. It is based on an admission that the utilitarian algorithm fails to yield a decision procedure that sorts every act into morally right, wrong or permitted. As such, it concedes that some actions may not be morally significant, but only when a determinate moral verdict is impossible to achieve. It makes an exception to the invasive tendency of morality not because that follows from its principles, but only by virtue of the necessity of allowing for ignorance. In addition, there will be some conditions under which the application of Rule Utilitarianism violates the Principle of Utility itself. That will happen, albeit infrequently, when a catastrophic consequence seems certain to result from following the rule. The problematic example of lying to save a life makes the point. A Kantian can rest their case for sticking to the rule on the unpredictability of consequences: the murderer might conceivably make a martyr of the unfortunate fugitive, which in turn would bring about a revolution leading to widespread and enduring benefits for all. Still, when the immediate ill effect of telling the truth is clear, most would decide that the rule is better ignored.

A utilitarian might be content to toggle between Rule and Act Consequentialism. A reasonable second-order principle might recommend acting on the basis of immediate effects whenever these can be reasonably predicted. When that is impossible, go with the rule.

That would amount to a third-order rule, based on the allegedly preferable consequences of obeying the second-order rule when and only when the first-order rule appears to give the wrong answer. That could be confusing, but need not be inconsistent. Inasmuch as it succeeds, however, it restores the original situation in which it seemed that there is a moral answer to every question, even when we are unable to discover it. In so doing, it undermines the hope of limiting the totalising encroachment of morality on every aspect of the observant utilitarian's life.

In response, the utilitarian can escape the charge of totalising by simply decreeing exceptions in practice. One way to do this is simply to declare, arbitrarily, that some choices are just too unimportant to matter. But that is just what I meant by the claim that to evade the charge of unreasonable totalisation, utilitarian theory must resort to arbitrary limitations on the scope of its own fundamental principle.

One more move is available to the utilitarian who wants to deny the relevance of some forms of pleasure or distress. There might be some reasons that can just be rejected outright as not worthy of consideration. That might be tempting when considering distress caused by repugnant forms of prejudice. It recalls John Stuart Mill's attempt to explain why we are inclined to think some pleasures less worthy of moral endorsement than others. Some people claim to be made physically uncomfortable by the proximity, or the undeniable achievements or prosperity, of members of groups they despise. Some have become enraged by the very thought that others were enjoying sexual pleasures they disapprove of, or by improvements in the standard of living of a group they despise.[5] The question for the utilitarian is this: what weight should be given to the distress caused in a bigot by their own prejudice?

You may well believe that the pain felt by a racist at a Black person's success, however genuine, may simply be ignored in the calculus of utility because it is in itself contemptible. But on strictly utilitarian grounds, it is not clear how 'being contemptible' should count in the calculation. Of course, the consequences of prejudice are among those that are easiest to assess. A utilitarian will have no trouble providing good utilitarian reasons to want to eliminate prejudice. To name but two: prejudice harms the mental and physical health of their victims, and causes economic inefficiency in the entire society. But that explanation does not connect with the intuition that some forms of distress simply do not deserve to be taken seriously as reasons. Here again, then, it seems that the Principle of Utility is subject to a kind of domestication that limits its range of application when its implications are just too implausible.

This last observation applies more generally whenever utilitarians want to set aside an area of personal freedom when it raises only questions of prudence rather than morality. Moral claims, it is generally held, outrank those of prudence, but surely whether to play hockey or chess, say, is not a moral question. These are all choices that would be rated as 'permitted'. It is not clear, however, that Utilitarianism can consistently insulate such questions from its own reach. Since your happiness is a component of the total, any harm you do to yourself will affect the net total. If hockey can harm you, your choosing to play it could strictly be immoral.

More generally, even if we ignore the intricacies suggested by phenomena like that of the butterfly effect, there are reasons to think that not even the trivial can in principle be kept apart from the morally significant. Peter Singer has stressed the inescapable fact that the price of an additional pair of shoes might save some distant child from starvation (Singer, 2009). For a consistent utilitarian, you are guilty whenever you contribute much less to charity than what would entail your own destitution. Since most people find this to be more than they can accept, Singer has provided a calculator that advises you on how much you should *reasonably* set aside to save others from poverty.[6] But that again sets an arbitrary limit to the Principle of Utility.

To be sure, we can understand that limit itself to be set on utilitarian principles. Too obsessive a preoccupation with the calculation of consequences and their utility takes time, and time is utils. That calculation tells you when it is counterproductive to calculate further. But it does not negate the theoretical point that the calculation one neglects would be relevant, if you could make it fast enough. Once equipped with the astounding capabilities of present and future AI, the calculation of ever more complex chains of consequence and their evaluations might come to seem feasible; and once feasible, it will be morally obligatory. The more we know, the less freedom morality will allow us. The prospect is chilling.

Let me now turn to Kantian Deontology. Is it any less invasive than Utilitarianism?

KANTIAN DEONTOLOGY

In constructing morality, Immanuel Kant undertook an extraordinary feat: to show that a system of moral duties and prohibitions can be derived, purely by logic, from the minimal assumption that you are capable of doing something deliberately. Here, to complement the sketch offered in the previous chapter, is a little more about how it is supposed to work.

Common sense would suggest that we espouse many conditional imperatives in ordinary life. Conditional imperatives are of the sort you might find in a recipe: if you want to make a soufflé, beat the egg whites with a whisk. The antecedent (the if-clause) of such a conditional refers to a potential goal. If that goal is one that is pursued by virtually everyone, such as continued existence, then it makes sense to endorse a general imperative, *keep hydrated*. The conditional, *If you want to survive, then keep hydrated*, can be left unspoken.

It is not a law of logic or even of biology that literally every living thing desires to survive. So even a widely applicable imperative is not strictly unconditional. Kant argues, however, that an absolute, unconditional imperative—a 'Categorical Imperative'—follows from the simple fact that you can act for a reason. Just as you can *just see*, as a rational being, that $2 + 2 = 4$, you are expected to just see that as an agent acting for *reasons*, you are *rational*. It is then supposed to follow that when considering whether to perform an act of type X, you can test for its status as forbidden, permissible or obligatory by asking whether, as a rational agent, you could coherently envisage a world in which it is a law of nature that everyone does X.

This test can be applied to any potential choice. According to Kant, it not only applies when my actions affect others, but explicitly burdens me with duties to myself. These include a prohibition against wasting my talents, neglecting my health or killing myself. Such duties or prohibitions might, of course, derive from the fact that the loss of my own health and life may affect others, but on Kant's theory, they hold regardless of any such effects. Even if we can imagine a situation in which my actions affect no one else, they cannot fail to affect me.

In a religious context, the concept of duties to myself makes sense. If I am God's creature, it is not absurd to suppose that he created me for purposes of his own, and that he alone is entitled to dispose of me as he sees fit. My primary duties would then be to God, and duties to myself could derive from that primary duty. God may decree that I should cultivate the capacities required for me to serve his ends.

But Kantian Deontology makes no appeal to God. It is supposed to derive purely from reason. As you might expect, Kant's defenders have deployed ingenious arguments in support of the implausible thesis that I cannot consistently desire to end my own life, or allow my talents to lie fallow. I shall not attempt to reconstruct or address those arguments. Suffice it to say that they have not been widely persuasive. The very idea of duties to myself makes little sense in secular terms. Sure, you might sometimes say I *promised myself* . . . But a promise can always be waived by its beneficiary. As the promisee, you can waive the promise, even if your past self has made it. All that takes is changing your mind. And while constancy is widely regarded as a virtue, and some individuals take pride in their constancy, it would not generally be prudent to insist on a duty never to change your mind.

Kantians recognise both 'perfect' and 'imperfect' duties. Perfect duties are strictly required (or may take the form of something's being strictly prohibited). The prohibitions against lying and suicide are perfect duties, respectively to others and to oneself. Imperfect duties are ones the fulfilment of which admits of degrees. You could always give more to charity, or do more to develop your talents. We recognise 'reasonable limits', to the demands of imperfect duties: we shan't blame you if you give less than you could, or spend less time than you might in the gym, practising the piano, or learning mathematics. Most people have several talents and some have many. The Categorical Imperative would also need to evaluate the importance of all my potential talents when I lack the time to develop them all. The precise point where we are to locate the acceptable minimum is arbitrary.

Some Kantians, perhaps even Kant himself, might grant that sometimes you can be justified in violating even a perfect duty: sometimes concern for others' welfare means that you really need to lie. But those concessions, however sensible, are not part of the Kantian system. On the contrary, any derogation from the Categorical Imperative is a violation. Much like the adjustments or exceptions accorded by a utilitarian to the duty to maximise utility, such a derogation is a concession to common sense, which is resistant to the totalising prospect of one's every act being a potential target of moral appraisal. Any intentional action is required, permitted or forbidden on the basis of the test of consistency set by the Categorical Imperative. Even when my action concerns only myself, I can never escape the watchful eye of Morality.

CONCLUSION: THE CHARGE IS SUSTAINED

In this chapter, I have tried to explain how two leading moral theories elaborated by philosophers tend to reinforce the widely shared psychological tendency to moralise—to drag everything we think, do or even feel into the moral spotlight. If you adopt one of those moral theories, you will at every turn find yourself a potential target of blame, for which guilt or shame must amend.

Perhaps this is to be welcomed. One powerful strand of Christian thought has always stressed that we are born stained with original sin, that our nature is fundamentally corrupt and that all of us should live in terror of eternal hellfire. Jonathan Bennett quotes a typical passage from eminent theologian and philosopher Jonathan Edwards (1703–1758). Edwards was famous for arguing that the idea of free will is incoherent, so that efforts to avoid God's wrath by doing good deeds were powerless anyway. Nevertheless, here's what he thought of you:

> The God that holds you over the pit of hell, much as one holds a spider or some loathsome insect over the fire, abhors you, and is dreadfully provoked; . . . he is of purer eyes than to bear to have you in his sight; you are ten thousand times so abominable in his eyes as the most hateful venomous serpent is in ours.
>
> (Quoted in Bennett, 1974, p. 128)

If that expresses your own view of your conspecifics, then you may welcome whatever restraining influence morality might have over them, and whatever dire punishment it might demand. Otherwise, you might find both the moralisation rampant on social media and the philosophers' confining moral edifices in the sky to be more vexatious than helpful.

This should not be interpreted as claiming that we should not scrutinise our actions and our motives, or that we should never judge an action to be mistaken, or seek for a more satisfactory way of defining and securing our goals. Rather, what I mean to encourage is the thought that such scrutiny does not need to be made under the intimidating aegis of Morality. We saw that the uses of words such as right, wrong, good and bad are as diverse as the topics of conversation we can raise or the things in which we can take an interest. And while it appears impossible to demarcate the domain of the moral in a way that would be compatible with morality's claim to universality, it is clear enough that we care about many other things, which morality urges us to demote. Aesthetic considerations play a huge part in what makes life worth living, for example. Caring about beauty is one of the very few traits that humans universally share (Dissanayake, 2000). Yet morality often requires us to relegate the beautiful to the status of mere tastes, trumped by and devalued from the moral point of view.

Wherever the line of demarcation is drawn, it is bound to leave much of the thought, feeling and enterprise we care about outside of its purview. Better to let all our reasons compete on an equal footing, rather than conferring a privileged status on the ones we call moral.

Two frameworks for reasons

We can never, even by the most strenuous self-examination, get to the bottom of our secret impulsions.

Immanuel Kant

An agent is judged worthy of moral praise or blame in the light of their reasons for acting. Morality must, therefore, presuppose that we can identify those reasons. In this chapter, I identify a general problem facing the identification of an agent's reasons. I argue that the explicit reasons we give are at best approximations of our causally effective reasons. Those approximations may be insufficiently accurate to justify a moral appraisal. That is because they are subject to systematic distortion of two sorts. The first is due to the inaccessibility to awareness of an agent's causally effective motivations: self-deception, and the inherent difficulty of self-knowledge, have often been discussed by psychologists from Sigmund Freud to contemporary cognitive scientists. The second is less often mentioned. It stems from the need to shed information when the underlying causal framework is translated into explicit reasons. Both factors are due to a more general difference between two modes of thinking, only one of which essentially involves language. As a result, the more accessible level of explicit practical reasons is often systematically inaccurate.

DOI: 10.4324/9781003278252-5

That two-tiered structure of our reasons—our causally effective motivations, and the explicit reasons we use in justifying what we do to ourselves and others—is familiar from both common lore and scientific literature. Put simply, it consists in the fact that you sometimes don't know what you really want. Philosophers have not sufficiently stressed the extent to which this familiar story undermines the project of moral appraisal. To introduce this two-tiered structure of reasons, let me contrast two ways of thinking about practical reasoning.

TWO MODELS OF DELIBERATION: THE ARISTOTELIAN VS THE BAYESIAN

Consider a simple case of means–end deliberation. This is what Aristotle regarded as a paradigm case:

> [I want to do what a man should do]
> Every man should take walks,
> I am a man,
> (Therefore) [I decide to take a walk.]
>
> (cf. Nussbaum, 1978, pp. 40)

This is supposed to illustrate how a decision is explained and justified by referring to a goal, want or desire, together with a relevant fact about the situation (here, that I am a man).

Obviously, while this bears some resemblance to what someone might say when asked why they did something, it is laughably unrealistic both as an explanation and as an account of deliberation. A slightly more realistic story might go like this:

> A walk would be good for me, but it's rainy and cold; besides, I have a lot of things to do. I can go tomorrow instead; anyway, I've been

walking quite a bit lately. Also I just don't really feel like it. Still,
I guess I will.

Even then, those considerations don't provide any genuine explanation for the behaviour engaged in, unless each of them is quantified. A walk would be good: but how good? It's rainy and cold: but how disagreeable is that? How urgent are those other things I must do? And so on. Once we know the strength of each of those causal factors, we can infer what the agent did. But that same list of factors, unquantified, could explain whatever they did, depending on those values. By contrast, the Aristotelian syllogism, if its premises are true, does claim to provide an explanation of the resulting behaviour. Although both the intensity of my desires and my confidence in the factual premises may vary, the design of the Aristotelian syllogism provides no convenient way of taking degrees into account. Unless we can do that, the syllogism can reflect the sequence of thoughts resulting in a deliberate decision, but it cannot specify the actual causal role played by each 'reason'.

Modern 'Bayesian' Decision Theory is designed to fill that lacuna. It explains behaviour more precisely by assigning degrees to both the agent's wants and their confidence in the relevant factual premises. It then calculates an action's 'expected utility' as the sum of the weighted utilities of each of its possible outcomes.[1]

Bayesian Decision Theory regards every decision we make as a gamble. For some decisions, only a high degree of confidence in the facts of the situation warrants the gamble. You risk your life when you cross the street, so you need to be highly confident that no car is close enough to hit you. By contrast, an exotic dish might be worth tasting even if you think you are highly unlikely to like it. It's not irrational to rely on an unlikely proposition, providing the payoff is high if it's true, and not too bad if it isn't.

That marks a radical difference between the conceptions of belief involved in the two models of deliberation. In a Practical Syllogism, the premises are typically asserted without specification of degree. At least one premise specifies a goal, something you want; and at least one premise specifies a proposition you are treating as true. The latter exemplifies the familiar way of talking about beliefs. You can usually say whether you believe that p, even if you hadn't been thinking about it. To say you believe it amounts to *assenting* to p. For this reason, I shall refer to Assent belief, or Abelief, when saying you believe something without qualification. An Abelief that p commits you to asserting p (unless you want to conceal your belief), to using p as a premise in arguments and to relying on it in explicit deliberation or justification. It's the kind of belief normally implied by a claim to know that p. When we speak of belief in this way, we may be more or less confident, but we don't think of it as admitting of any precise degree that requires to be taken into account in the course of deliberation or argument.

Abelief contrasts with what I shall call Probability belief or Pbelief, which is the kind of belief involved in any action considered as a gamble, as in Bayesian Decision Theory. Pbelief is a measure of subjective probability;[2] it lies in a range from 1, absolute certainty, to 0, the certainty that p is false. In Bayesian Decision Theory, degrees of desire then combine with Pbeliefs to explain and/or justify a particular decision. Unlike the Practical Syllogism, which deals in unqualified desires and Abeliefs, Bayesian Theory takes into account degrees of both desires and beliefs (as Pbeliefs), and represents the organism's computation of each potential action's expected utility.

Some important differences emerge from a comparison of the role of Abelief in the Practical Syllogism and that of Pbelief in Bayesian Decision Theory. Both might be used to explain and justify. But the Bayesian model does not require an agent to have conscious access to the exact degree of their Pbeliefs. The Aristotelian model, by contrast, uses the agent's explicit Abeliefs. For the purposes of moral appraisal, in particular, an agent's explicit reasons are typically our best evidence as to the nature of their intentional actions. They are the target of moral judgments justifying praise or blame. Accurate assessments of an agent's reasons are therefore presupposed by moral judgment.

Such accurate assessments, however, are difficult, if not impossible, given the discrepancy between the two sorts of belief as well as the differences between their roles in the two rival models of action explanation. Inasmuch as we rely on what people say about their own reasons, we seem to have a clear view of what they are up to. Sometimes we don't believe what they say, judging them to be hypocritical or self-deceived. But our own insight into others' motives isn't always reliable either, especially when just observing their behaviour without knowing the complex biographical details that led them to it. So we can seldom be certain of having correctly assessed the causally effective reasons of their actions.

More generally, there are two impediments to knowledge of causally effective reasons. The first is the relative inaccessibility to consciousness just noted of beliefs and desires posited by Bayesian Theory. The second is that even if we assume that we can represent the latter accurately, their translation into the explicit reasons used in practical syllogisms may involve a loss of information. To explain these two reasons, I must make a brief detour.

DUAL PROCESS THEORY

It is an odd fact that while the evidence shows that animals, including humans, act on probabilities in the way described by Bayesian Theory, we are very poor at articulating those probabilities. This is only a specific aspect of a general truth about our own access to our mental states. The method of psychoanalysis, formulated a century ago by Sigmund Freud (1856–1939), stressed the extent to which we are ignorant of our own motivations. Although Freud gets little respect nowadays, experimental psychology has amply confirmed that insight. When an agent is challenged to provide a reason for a decision they can't account for, they simply confabulate (Hirstein, 2005). They invent reasons that seem plausible in the light of what are taken to be common explanations for the behaviour in question. In a classic experiment, for example, subjects asked to choose between (actually identical) items of clothing tended to pick those on their right. Since that is clearly irrelevant in the light of common sense, subjects invented some imaginary advantage, citing colour or fabric quality, which they attributed to the items chosen (Nisbett & Wilson, 1977).

In short, the mechanisms underlying most of what we do are inaccessible to the language-speaking conscious mind. This is partly explained by the architecture of attention. Our explicit awareness affords us an extraordinarily narrow 'work space', which has been estimated to contain no more than a handful of distinct items that can command attention at one time (Miller, 1956). (We don't notice this because we cheat by chunking: distinct objects form patterns that then reappear as single items, allowing us to contemplate highly complex patterns and relationships.) Despite this, we respond in complex ways to many features of our environment at any one waking moment. Only occasionally are the relevant features brought to awareness.

All this is quite obvious once we pay attention to it: most of what we do and think is due to efficient mechanisms, the workings of which are unknown to us. Think of all the amazing things you do without thought or effort: recall information, recognise the validity of an argument, catch a ball. You generally have no idea how you did those things. Your response is intuitive, fast and effortless. By contrast, if you are asked to make your reasoning explicit—if you had to show the calculation that led you to expect the ball in the location where you will catch it, for example—you will find it difficult, slow and effortful, and usually quite impossible without pen and paper or calculator. These two modes of thinking can be described as respectively 'intuitive' and 'analytic'. They are now widely referred to as System 1 and System 2 in the extensive literature devoted to 'Dual Process Theory' (Evans, 2018; Kahneman, 2011). (See Box #4.)

The intuitive system S1 does not need to work with language. But it does much of our thinking as well as that of other animals without language. Animal behaviour, as well as the human brain's control of physical motion when it is adapting to changing conditions in real time, has been shown to fit nicely with Bayesian Theory (Yu, 2007). It is therefore reasonable to assume that Bayesian deliberation is implemented in the brain as an S1 process. On that assumption, we can expect Pbeliefs to enter into the explanation of behaviour even when we would not say that the agent 'believes' the propositions in question. If that is right, it is reasonable to conclude that Bayesian Theory provides as accurate an explanatory framework as we could wish for the process of decision as performed by S1.

> **BOX #4 DUAL PROCESS THEORY**
>
> Dual Process Theory is a psychological framework that proposes humans have two distinct cognitive processes or systems involved in decision making and information processing.
>
> System 1, often described as the intuitive or automatic system, operates effortlessly and rapidly, often below the threshold of awareness. It relies on heuristics, associations and previous experiences to make judgments and decisions. It is responsible for our immediate reactions, emotional responses and intuitive judgments. It guides our everyday actions and helps us navigate familiar situations efficiently.
>
> System 2 is the reflective or analytic system. It is slow, deliberate, and involves conscious effort. Its province includes logical reasoning, explicit argument and deliberation. It is responsible for complex problem solving, critical thinking and evaluating the outcomes of decisions. Unlike System 1, System 2 thinking requires attention. As I interpret it, it also requires linguistic syntax and logic, including mathematics.
>
> Dual Process Theory recognises that the two systems interact, but the relative influence of each can vary depending on context and individual differences. In some situations, System 1 might dominate, leading to quick and instinctive responses. When System 2 is engaged, it generates explicit, careful and deliberate reasoning.
>
> One key claim of Dual Process Theory, which in popular discussion is perhaps over-emphasised, is that System 1 thinking is prone to biases and errors. While it offers efficiency and speed, it can lead to cognitive biases, snap judgments and reliance on stereotypes. And indeed, when the issues facing an agent are ones for which natural selection and early learning cannot have prepared them, System 2 is required to overcome these biases by engaging in deeper analysis and critical thinking. Nevertheless, most of what we do is done, highly efficiently, by System 1.

Estimating degrees of Pbelief

If reasons, and notably the subjective probabilities represented by Pbelief, are largely inaccessible to consciousness, how could we measure them?

The answer is to be found along lines suggested by Frank Ramsey (1903–1930) in his original formulation of subjective probability as degree of belief (Ramsey, 1990). It goes something like this.

Most of the time, we can tell when an agent—a person or another animal—is frustrated. This allows us to infer that agents often succeed in doing what they try to do. That suggests that what agents choose reflects what they want and believe. If so, it should be possible, at least in theory, to estimate the subjective probabilities and desirabilities ascribed by an agent to various states of affairs.

Start by assuming that beliefs and desires (in the broad sense in which I have been using these terms) make sense of what an agent does. Beliefs and desires 'rationalise' the behaviour— they make it intelligible as something a rational agent would do. (See Box #3 in Chapter 4.) In any given case, there may be many possible ways of fitting reasons to behaviour. If S walks out of the house with an umbrella, S may expect rain and want to stay dry; or they may think the umbrella looks cool; or they may expect sunshine and want protection from UV rays. And so on—with, of course, all desires as well as expectations coming in degrees. We need to pare down the possibilities, lest we be faced with an unmanageable plethora of ambiguous cases. That requires careful observation of S's behaviour over a period of time. We will need to detect patterns from which we can extract a workable theory about S's wants and Pbeliefs. Even then the method may mislead, for a discrepancy might signal a misunderstanding by the observer, a genuine incoherence on the part of S or merely a change of mind in S. Inconstancy is not inconsistency. Unless the agent can talk, and answer questions explicitly, mistakes and ambiguities may remain unavoidable.

Expert animal trainers dispense with talk and do this sort of thing all the time (Grandin & Johnson, 2005). And experimental psychologists, with their customary ingenuity, might devise crucial tests to diagnose which of two prospective outcomes an agent preferred, and even, given their observed preferences, what probability they must be assigning to relevant propositions to best account for their choice. With agents capable of speech, Ramsey suggested posing hypothetical wagers, the acceptance or rejection of which (based on the gambler's spontaneous S1-type intuition rather than to any S2 calculation) would reveal even their unarticulated Pbeliefs. If an agent is consistently indifferent between betting for or against p with odds of 5/1 against (like getting a 6 on a single roll of a die), for example, it would indicate that their degree of belief in p is 1/6.

As will be obvious, these ways of measuring Pbeliefs are neither easy nor reliable. That confirms that our real Bayesian reasons will often remain inaccessible. The mere possibility of such measurements will not be of much comfort to the moralist who wants to ground moral judgment on an accurate assessment of the agent's reasons. For while inferences to such assessments are possible, they are rarely achieved in practice. The ascription of reasons for an agent's actions, which is crucial for a fair moral assessment, would often remain out of reach. For the moralist, that is an obstacle. For the amoralist, it is merely a null answer to a question that presupposes mythical facts.

Abelief involves a loss of information

I now come to the second reason for saying that the duality of Pbelief and Abelief undermines moral evaluation.

When we justify a decision by appeal to reasons, these will generally be formulated as Abeliefs, unmodified by degrees. If I am right in suggesting that the causally effective beliefs involved in true reasons are Pbeliefs, the formulation of a justification will involve moving to a state of Abelief that p from a high degree of Pbelief. This does not require the Pbelief to have been conscious. Supposing it could be made explicit, however, the translation from Pbelief to Abelief could sometimes entail a loss of crucial information.

To see why, consider a simple example. You will take an umbrella when going out only if you believe that p, where p is *that it will rain today*, and believing is understood as Abelieving, of the sort that can figure in a Practical Syllogism. Suppose the weather forecast is your evidence E. You start with a Pbelief in p *given* E, a conditional probability relative to your evidence, which can be expressed as $Prob(p/E)$. From here, getting to an Abelief that p requires at least two steps, each of which involves throwing away some information.

(i) At the first step, you need to detach an unqualified probability $Prob(p)$ from the conditional probability $Prob(p/E)$, thus discarding the information that this value was relative to a given evidence E. The discarded information is important, because if you have ignored a competing forecast, your inference to the unconditional probability might prove hasty. By discarding the provenance of the unconditional probability $Prob(p)$, you are taking on an extra risk of error in your estimate of your own belief.

(ii) You now have a free-standing Pbelief, Prob(p). A second step is needed to take you from that to an unqualified Abelief that p. This second step is momentous: for no degree of probability is always sufficient to license an unqualified Abelief (*Ichikawa & Steup, 2018). The improbable is sometimes true: that is what sells lottery tickets. So your inference to an Abelief must be based on more than just the high value of your Pbelief. But whatever that value, as well as whatever additional factors led you to adopt the unqualified Abelief that It will rain, both are also lost once you take that second step. As a result, even if you had the best possible access to the underlying layer of subjective desires and beliefs, your best estimate of your reason, let alone anyone else's, is only an evidentially impoverished approximation of the reason that actually motivated you.

So far in this chapter, I have contrasted unqualified wants and Abeliefs with quantified desirabilities and Pbeliefs. Abeliefs, I have argued, are at two removes from an agent's 'real' reasons. The actual determinants of behaviour are Pbeliefs, of which the translation to verbalised Abeliefs may have resulted in a loss of information in two ways. Abeliefs, produced for public view and moral assessment, can therefore be less accurate in their expression of the agent's true reasons than Pbeliefs, but Pbeliefs can't confidently be invoked because they are not generally available to the agent's awareness. To be sure, your Abelief is itself likely to influence your Pbelief in some measure; but that merely adds to indeterminacy and does not solve the problem. As a pertinent meme wisely puts it, you shouldn't believe everything you think—even if you can't help being influenced by what you think you believe.

Abeliefs are involved in explicit verbal assertions and arguments. They play a key role in the reasons for action that are the basis of moral appraisal. But even when Abeliefs represent an agent's sincere attempt to provide reasons, those Abeliefs are likely to be inaccurate. They are at best approximations of the Pbeliefs that are the effective causal factors driving action. It follows, then, that even if we could successfully demarcate the moral domain from the aesthetic and the prudential, and even if there were a consensus on moral rules, we could not be confident of correctly ascribing moral responsibility. That would seem to be a serious impediment to any moralist proposing to evaluate the moral worth of any action.

To an amoralist, by contrast, the inaccessibility of more precise Pbeliefs and the resulting inaccuracy of Abeliefs, pose no special problem beyond the inevitable uncertainty of our understanding of ourselves and others. For the amoralist is committed to withholding any moral judgments that would require them to pinpoint an agent's authentic reasons. Once again, the amoralist's rejection of the need for moral assessment dispenses them from having to attempt an impossible calculation. To one whose judgment of an agent does not depend on a moral appraisal of that agent's motivation, the impossibility of assessing moral responsibility is of no concern. An observer can like or dislike a given act solely on the basis of their own assessment of the act's nature and consequences. Such an observer can even confidently judge the act to have been irrational, for the basis for a verdict of irrationality depends on what the agent *says* about their wants and aims, not on what they are observed to *do*. By contrast, when we are observing the behaviour of a non-language-using animal, a charge of irrationality can never be sustained. For such a charge must *assume* that the agent harbours specific Abeliefs and explicit aims or wants. But animals without language don't have Abeliefs; and as for those who can speak, it is only the moralist who needs to delve into the act's causal antecedents in the agent's own mind.

What binds a reason-to-X to the act of doing X?

The moralist might still complain that only a *value*, whether moral or of some other kind, can provide a *reason* to act. How could an ordinary, non-moral and non-normative fact be a reason to do anything? Here is a modest suggestion.

At first sight, on the basis of its syntax, *R is a reason to do A* looks like a two-place relation, holding between R and the action A that is rationalised by R. But that is too simple and not at all explanatory. In accordance with the commonsense assumption that we act on beliefs and desires, we can understand R as involving at least two variables, one corresponding to belief (B) and the other to desire (D), that constitute a reason for the decision X. So a reason to do X would be, at the very least, a three-place relation linking B, D and X.

But a second look reveals that this can't be quite right.

That a desire for X is an essential component of a reason to pursue X is a grain of insight contained in the Aristotelian Practical Syllogism: if I want X and A would result in X, then (other things being equal) I have reason to do A. Even if X turns out to be bad for me, my desire represents it as good for me, and that is part of my reason to pursue it.

But a reason to pursue something desired is not yet a reason to do anything specific about it. As Aristotle's skeletal schema illustrates, having a reason to do something specific in pursuit of a goal requires the agent to take stock of the relevant facts about their situation. That's the Belief part of the three-part relation. It can't be quite right, however, to assimilate that second component of my reason to my beliefs. Recall the paradigm:

P1 I want to do what a man should do.
P2 Every man should take walks,
P3 I am a man,
(Therefore) [I decide to take a walk.]

Notice that the second and third premises *express* beliefs, but do not *mention* any belief. While my belief that P2 and P3 are true contributes to the *causation* of my decision, my *reason* is not my psychological state but the objective fact that the act envisaged will secure my goal. The role of my psychological state of belief is to plug in the *fact* that constitutes my reason into the black box that processes the algorithm resulting in my decision. If I was mistaken about that 'fact', then I was mistaken in thinking that I had a reason. My belief still caused me to act, but my act was not, after all, justified.

To make this clear, it will help to recall the difference between the explanatory and the justificatory function of a reason. For the former, only the internal states of the agent are pertinent. For it is the agent's psychological states of belief and desire that are causally responsible for their behaviour. That is true whether their belief is true or not, and regardless of whether what they want is good for them. More is required for the belief component of a reason to succeed in justifying an action than is needed to explain it. If a reason adduced in the first person is to successfully justify the action (without importing non-existent normative facts), it must consist only in natural facts. In the premise that expresses desire, the relevant natural fact is still the psychological brute fact of the agent's desire. On the side of belief, by contrast, the relevant fact is not the agent's belief, but *the fact that doing A will likely bring about X*. Only those facts can contribute to that agent's justifying reason. For unless the agent's belief were required to be true, every action would be trivially justified. An action motivated by absurd or fantastical beliefs would be as fully justified as a perfectly rational one.

With those clarifications in mind, we can characterise more precisely the relation between a reason and the action it rationalises. It relates two kinds of objective facts to the agent's action: an objective fact about a relevant situation and an objective fact about the agent's goals or desires. There is no need for any objective *normative* fact, value or ought-statement. The agent's desire is a fact about them. The actual situation, i.e., the fact that A would be conducive to X, provides the affordance. Both are non-normative, natural facts, and their status as reasons is attested simply by the truth of the conditional imperative of the type *If you want to cook an egg, heat the pan*. In this case, for example, the purely factual truth in play is the fact that under the circumstances heating the pan is a necessary means to cooking the egg.

To be sure, not every action can be understood in terms of simple means–end reasoning. Something of the longer story that must be told to explain the cases that involve what a community of speakers agree to call 'values' will be addressed in Chapter 6. For the moment, though, this is enough to conclude that explanation by reasons does not necessarily require normative facts. A reason can consist in one or more natural facts. Practical reasoning links such facts about the world to action, when one of those facts is about the agent's want or goal, and the other is about the likely result of that type of action under these circumstances.

The next chapter further explores the nature of reasons purporting to be moral reasons. Moral reasons, in contrast with those I refer to as natural reasons, are held to be inherently normative. I will be arguing that if, as is widely taken for granted by moral theorists, all moral properties supervene on non-moral properties, then the labelling of some properties as moral or immoral amounts to an illegitimate form of double counting. This problem is rendered particularly acute, given the two-tiered structure of reasons just reviewed. For if what I have argued in this chapter is right, then the natural properties on which moral ones supervene are already simplified duplicates, verbally articulated, of the effective reasons identified by Bayesian Decision Theory.

Buy one, get one free.

Supermarket promotion

Reasons to act come in a host of different kinds. They can be driven by impulsive whims or by long-term concerns; they can relate to my own welfare or that of others; and they can pertain to any domain, from the aesthetic to the financial. Only some are deemed *moral*; those, we are taught, trump all other types of reasons. At the same time, as I shall explain in a moment, moral reasons are held to depend in a specific way on ordinary reasons. Suppose doing X will cause someone pain. That may strike you as a reason to refrain from doing X. That, moralists will tell you, 'grounds' *another* reason not to do X, namely that doing so would be *immoral*. So now it looks like you have two reasons to refrain from X instead of one: first, *that X will cause pain*, and second, *that X is immoral*. But since this second reason was 'grounded' in the first, what can it add to it? What justifies this sort of double counting, and what entitles it to override other, 'non-moral', reasons?

THICK AND THIN CONCEPTS

To look at this more closely, we first need to dispose of a potential objection to the very idea that a fact or situation can always be described in some neutral way, without any

DOI: 10.4324/9781003278252-6

implication of moral approval or disapproval. Some thinkers have claimed that some natural facts are sometimes loaded with inherent moral significance from which they cannot be pried apart. In one form, that claim is based on the feeling of obviousness that attends such judgments as 'it is wrong to torture innocent children'. But it is also sometimes bolstered by invoking so-called 'thick' concepts, a notion that was introduced in the pertinent sense by the British philosopher Bernard Williams (1929–2003). Thick concepts combine descriptive content with a moral assessment (*Väyrynen, 2021). If thick concepts are indispensable and their descriptive content cannot be dissociated from their moral force, then an amoralist would have to deprive themself of a significant part of English vocabulary. That might be too high a price to pay for amoralism. As we shall see, however, that sacrifice will not be needed.

For some thick concepts, it is easy to separate the fact from the evaluation. A murder, for example, is not a mere killing but a *wrongful* killing. 'Killing' is the appropriate word if one does not want to convey the negative moral (and legal) judgment implicit in the word 'murder'. The descriptive content, *causing death*, can be detached from its assessment as wrongful. In the case of other thick concepts, separating the descriptive from the evaluative element can seem more difficult. Some expressions, like 'generous', 'kind' and 'cruel', come with only loose criteria for their application. Yet both hearer and speaker will generally agree, providing they come from similar social circles, about what counts as generous, kind or cruel. Without such background agreement, disentangling the word's descriptive content from its evaluative force may be hard.

Consider two examples: 'cruel' and 'tactful'. A tactful remark is one that delicately avoids some reference to a sensitive issue that might cause discomfort. Cruelty involves the deliberate infliction of suffering. In each case, a detailed description of the action in context might not suffice to show why it is worthy of praise or blame unless speaker and audience share expectations and attitudes. Just today, as I write, the Economist notes that sending children to a boarding school at the age of seven or eight was once regarded as a mark of upper-class privilege. Nowadays, experts regard the practice as cruel. To ascribe a thick concept, one needs to be familiar with the attitudes of those who are using it. Members of a cohesive social group are bound by shared normative expectations, often derived from a common perception of social status. So, for example, expectations may be driven by the participants' recognition of deference due to an employer from a servant, to a teacher from student, or to a judge from an attorney. Social life depends at every turn on the participants' awareness of such things.

Expectations can be merely predictive, as when we expect summer weather to be warm. But when social relations are involved, what is expected is often regarded as what *ought* to occur: it is then viewed as *normative*. When such expectations are not shared, misunderstandings can give rise to offence. What was intended as a tactful remark, for example, may be heard as offensive evasion or disconcerting irrelevancy.

The normativity in social expectations is sometimes moral and sometimes not. How can we tell? As always, the answer seems to depend on who's around. Etiquette is not morality, but in some circles neglect of etiquette might be an offence that varies in gravity all the way to *lèse-majesté* punishable by death. Once again, the difficulty of demarcation might incline one to relativism. Moral or not, though, the shared normative expectations of social life need not make it impossible to disentangle evaluative from descriptive components of a thick concept. We may not be able to formulate all the normative implications and all the descriptive content of an expression precisely. But we can plausibly devise a story within which the evaluative force of the expression in question is reversed or annulled.

To see how, note first that the normative aspects of thick concepts are based on fine distinctions of degree. Often, as Aristotle pointed out, the virtuous response lies in the mean between extremes of insufficiency and excess. Disregarding risk counts as courageous only when it is judicious, but there is no strict line between the courageous and the reckless. Second, recall that the valence expressed by a thick concept depends on subtle background conditions, which are relied on even if they are not articulated. If some of those assumptions are not shared, the participants can reverse or annul the usual valence.

Return, for example, to the word 'tactful'. Without any change in what is said or in any of the objective circumstances making up its context, the utterance praised by one observer as tactful might be deplored by another as a mealy-mouthed reluctance to confront a touchy superior. Or consider cruelty, but suppose both speaker and hearer are sadists. They do not share the usual reluctance to cause harm. In that case, they might use the word 'cruel' in a sense that preserves its descriptive content, applicable to the gratuitous infliction of pain for the agent's own pleasure. For them, however, the word would carry no negative valence, since both approve of what most would condemn. Both interlocutors might agree that what they are doing is cruel, but regard that description as praise rather than disapproval.

A couple of examples do not establish a general truth. Still, it seems likely that this thought experiment can be generalised. I suspect that we could make up a similar story to reverse the valence carried by any thick concept, without any modification of its descriptive content. Thick concepts, while undoubtedly convenient in packaging description and evaluation together, do not preclude our prying apart their purely descriptive content from their evaluative connotation.

If that is right, it follows that where there is a moral disagreement, there must be some purely descriptive term, D, that both sides would agree fits the act in dispute. The disagreement concerns the attitude taken towards D: to some, D will seem self-evidently wrong, while those on the other side will no less confidently regard D as right or permissible. One side or the other may appeal to features of the context; the disagreement will then shift to the relevance of those features as reasons. Institutional facts might be cited, to which again the two sides may have different attitudes. In the end, though, attitudes and facts can be unscrambled.

A stark example that all too often figures in the news concerns so-called 'honour killings'. When a woman who has been raped is killed by her father or brother, the killing is not denied. Rather, its perpetrators invoke a conception of honour on which it was a duty they could not evade. An observer from a WEIRD culture will see things differently. The difference will be tied to the assumptions that each party takes for granted. On one side, a woman cannot be justifiably sanctioned for an act she did not intend. On the killers' side, the victim is sometimes accused of having provoked or willingly participated in the transgression. But more often the difference between the two cultures' conceptions of what is morally right and wrong extends to deeply embedded presuppositions about the nature of responsibility and desert. Where honour killing is condoned, the victim's personal responsibility is irrelevant. What she has endured, even if wholly against her will, has brought 'dishonour' to the family, and the 'impurity' must be cleansed.

Once those presuppositions on each side are taken for granted, the killing—a neutral description in itself—acquires a new thick descriptor. It could carry a positive or negative spin, as redeeming dishonour, or a negative one, as murder.

MORAL APPROVAL OR DISAPPROVAL IS ALWAYS AN ADD-ON

I conclude that any action or event can in principle be captured by a normatively neutral description. You or I will likely form attitudes of liking or disliking, approval or disapproval, towards those natural facts. But from the logical point of view, moral approval or condemnation is always an add-on. It does not correspond to a normative fact, because there are no normative facts for anything to correspond to.

To illustrate how an action neutrally described might give rise to a specifically *moral* attitude, consider the act of inserting ink through a person's epidermis into the papillary layer. Suppose Robin regards the fact that such an act might cause pain as a reason to refrain from it. That reason might be overridden if the pain is incurred by a client who asked Robin to give them a tattoo. The original reason still exists, but is outweighed. Now suppose that Robin merely wants to take sadistic pleasure in the infliction of pain. If Robin also *cares* about not inflicting gratuitous pain, they will have a reason to refrain. If not, Robin will indulge their sadistic impulse. But when the moralist adduces a further reason, namely that causing gratuitous pain is immoral, what if anything is added to the original reason to refrain?

If the label 'moral' did add to the original reason, it might do so in one of two ways. One would be to identify the original reason as belonging to a privileged class, which automatically confers priority to its members. That would require that we have a criterion for membership of the privileged class. It returns us to the need for a principle of demarcation, which, as we have seen, cannot be done to the satisfaction of all. In addition, even if we succeeded in demarcating the moral domain, we would still need to justify that domain's peculiar privilege.

A related strategy, which may or may not amount to the same thing, would be to claim that the label 'moral' does not merely qualify or categorise the original reason, but results in the existence of an entirely new reason, one that now trumps any other standing reason. This second formulation, I shall argue, is suggested by what philosophers generally agree is the relationship of 'supervenience' that holds between moral properties (either evaluative or deontic) and the natural properties that ground them. But when we look at what supervenience involves, it appears to be no more than a way of counting the same reason twice.

INTERNAL AND EXTERNAL

Before I explain this, we need to revisit an ambiguity in the claim that a subject S *has a reason* R to do or to refrain from doing something. We saw in the last chapter that philosophers have distinguished 'internalist' from 'externalist' readings of this phrase. While those expressions have been read in several ways in the context of different debates (*Finlay &

Schroeder, 2017), the central intuition behind the distinction is this. An externalist construal of the claim that R is a reason to do A for S implies nothing about S's awareness of the reason or its relevance. On that reading, it may be true at any time that I have all kinds of reasons to act or to believe, of which I remain unaware. By contrast, an internalist reading is one that requires S to be aware of R.

Here is the classic example. S is thirsty and believes that the glass placed before them contains a refreshing cocktail. From the internalist point of view, S has a reason to drink from the glass. But the glass is filled with a deadly poison. The externalist would then say that S has a very good reason to refrain from drinking, even though S is unaware of it. R is a reason for S (externally) because S would view it as a reason (internally) if they became aware of it.

Even if S is aware of R, however, an internalist might still deny that R must be a reason for S. For S might simply not care. When told that the glass contains a fatal dose of fertiliser rather than a refreshing cocktail, S might also happen to have been looking for a convenient way to end their life. In that case, R is not a reason for S. A Kantian, for whom suicide is always morally wrong, might admit that R is not functioning as a reason for S, yet still insist that it *ought* to.

The distinction between internalist and externalist conceptions of reasons has led to disputes about which should be regarded as our *real* reasons. Clearly, however, which construal is to be preferred depends entirely on the context in which it is brought up. In the example given, the belief that the glass contains a refreshing drink explains why the agent wants to drink it. That is the internalist view. But an externalist would be right to draw the agent's attention to the glass's actual content, for it is undoubtedly the sort of thing an agent would want to take into account.

My aim in bringing up that ambiguity here was to forestall any worry that it might affect my argument. A moment's reflection will be enough to show that the problem of double counting arises on either reading whenever it is appropriate. For it stems from the relation of dependence that holds between a putative normative reason and its natural ground or base. This is the case whether the reason is regarded from the externalist or the internalist point of view. In particular, it is widely agreed among philosophers that moral judgments 'supervene' on non-moral properties. To make this clear, let me clarify how this relation of 'supervenience' is to be understood.

SUPERVENIENCE

The basic idea is easy to explain. A property of type A supervenes on a property of type B if an item's possession of the supervening (type-A) property depends in a specific way on that item's possession of a type-B property. What is specific to the sort of dependency in question is this: the base (type-B) property can change without there being any change in the supervening (type-A) property, but the A-type property cannot change without a change in its B-type base.

Here is an example that does not involve moral terms. Whether a pattern is symmetrical depends on the spatial disposition of its physical or topographical features—its lines, shapes and colours. But as there are many ways of being symmetrical, a pattern's physical characteristics or base properties could change without affecting the pattern's degree of symmetry. The latter (the supervening property), however, could not be different without some change in the lines, shapes or colours (the base properties).

Now moral properties are commonly said to supervene on non-moral facts. For example, stealing is morally wrong, and stealing *consists* in taking something under certain specific condition—for example, (roughly) that the item taken belongs to someone else. That S took something that did not belong to them is the base event, on which S's being morally guilty supervenes. The property of moral wrongness is ascribed on the basis of the act's non-moral or natural property (the item's having been taken under the specified conditions).

It is easy to see that the two classes of properties are indeed related in the specified way: S would still be guilty of thieving if they stole something else. But they could not be absolved from the charge of thievery unless the underlying natural facts were different from what they were originally claimed to be.

Thus, once we separate the natural from the normative content of the thick concept (thievery), the latter supervenes on the former in the light of shared normative presuppositions.

This is generally true of any ought or value statement. Some true description of the situation in purely factual terms must explain and justify the moral claim. If moral claims supervene on natural facts, it follows that whenever two events or actions are identical in their non-moral properties, their moral properties must also be identical (*McPherson, 2019). From the point of view of a system of morality, complete knowledge of the non-moral properties of a given action is therefore sufficient to determine its moral properties.

DOUBLE COUNTING

This, then, is what I mean by double counting. In the last chapter, I argued that natural facts referred to in the conditional imperative that constitutes an agent's reason can be sufficient to explain or justify an action conforming to the consequent of that conditional. The natural fact that some act would hurt another person can both explain and justify refraining from it. But these same facts are also said to 'ground' an additional moral reason. The same facts are therefore being used as a reason twice over.

To see how this works in a little more detail, recall the distinction between explanation and justification. From the third-person point of view, the point of saying that an agent acted for a reason is to explain the agent's action. In this usage, the words 'reason' and 'cause' are often used interchangeably. If the reason you stopped at a service station on the highway was that you were hungry, it would be equally appropriate to say that hunger causally explained why you stopped. In the first person, the same phrase is commonly used not merely to explain but also to justify. The two uses of 'reason' are understood as referring to 'motivating' and 'normative' reasons respectively. In the latter case, the question 'Why did you stop?' can be taken as a challenge, amounting to 'What was the point of stopping?' as opposed to 'What was the psychological cause of your decision to stop?'

When what is in question is moral justification, as opposed to psychological causation—particularly but not exclusively when the reason is appealed to by the agent in the first person—the appeal to a reason is complicated by the fact that what seems to justify something in the eyes of the speaker may not justify it in the mind of the listener. Whether or not something counts as an *adequate* justifying reason can be contentious. Why-questions and their answers may form long chains. Why do X? To bring about Y. Why bring about Y? Because Y will promote Z. Etc. But in any given conversation, the chain will tend to end somewhere, not merely because of the participants' exhaustion, but because that final answer will seem obviously successful as an appropriate justification. But what marks that appropriate stopping point?

While that question can arise for any chain of justification, the answer is especially contentious when the 'moral' worth of an action is at issue. Was a gift truly motivated by a generous impulse, prompted by love and concern for the recipient's well-being? Or was it merely a case of 'virtue signalling', intended to boost your reputation and earn a tax deduction? We have seen how that observation rests on a deep feature of our human consciousness, involving two ways of understanding belief—Pbelief and Abelief—as well as two modes of mental functioning—intuitive and analytic. What these features of the mind explain is something that psychologists as well as novelists have long known: how easily we can be self-deceived.

Some cases of self-deception may be all too obvious, shading into conscious hypocrisy. We then say that the agent offered a rationalisation rather than reason.[1] A rationalisation is a reason that would have justified the action if it had motivated it, but that actually played no causal role in bringing it about. In such cases, the difference between motivation and justification becomes particularly stark. A successful justification must also be motivating; but an actual motivating reason may fail to justify.

THE MEANINGS OF GOOD

In other words, not all that seems to be good for you is actually so. Many thinkers agree that when we want something, we necessarily want it 'in the guise of the good'. But since we sometimes want things that will harm us, also in the guise of the good, we must distinguish *prima facie* or 'at first sight' desires from 'all things considered' desires. At any moment, any number of actions may strike you as good or desirable in some respect. Any uncompelled choice is presumed to have been made 'in the guise of the good'.

But 'good' is a notoriously tricky word (Kraut, 2012). To say that some X is a good X is not like saying that some X is a green X—for example, that this leaf is a green leaf. The latter can be decomposed into two propositions: this item is a leaf, and it is green. There is not a special way for a leaf to be green, different from the way that a boat or a book is green. All share the property of being green, which can be recognised even without knowing exactly what a leaf, a boat or a book is. The case of 'good' is different: a good boat and a good book share no property identifiable independently of the kind of things they are. To know what makes a good boat, you need to know what boats are for. Qualities that make for a good book make no sense if ascribed to a boat. And what a good leaf might be is obscure, unless there is some specific use that you want the leaf for.

Indeed, despite the enormous importance that the idea of The Good has had in the history of philosophy, there is really no such thing as The Good. Paul Ziff (1920–2003), having devoted a whole book to the question, came to the deflationary conclusion that 'good' just means 'answering to certain interests' (Ziff, 1960). The interests in question must be inferred from one's understanding of the point or purpose of the item to which goodness is being attributed. Thus, what makes a good boat, a good book or a good leaf depends entirely on what is wanted from a boat, a book or a leaf. Anything good is good as a thing of its kind, for something, or for someone (*Schroeder, 2021).

The 'guise of the good' must therefore be understood in terms of interests implied in any given context. Only sentient beings can have interests (although a sentient being could take an interest in anything). In a universe devoid of any sentient beings, nothing could be good or bad, except in a sense devoid of valence or normativity. One could perhaps use the word to draw attention to a causal dependency, meaning 'conducive to'. Some set of conditions C, for example, could be said to be good for the formation of a black hole. But if there were no beings capable of *caring*, there would be no interests to be answered to.

In our own world, the interests of sentient beings create reasons to act and to care. But since there are no moral facts, that does not automatically create moral reasons *in addition* to those that derive simply from our carings and wantings.

If we ignore the moral layer that results from double counting and just consider a reason to act, we are typically contemplating three things: first, some actual situation; second, a non-existent situation that appears desirable in the light of our wants; and third, potential actions that seem likely to bring about the situation envisaged. If they are to motivate you, your reasons must be internal: the interests to which what seems good answers must be your own.

To forestall misunderstanding, I hasten to repeat that your own interests are not confined to your 'self-interest'. Someone who truly cared about nothing but themselves, a pure egoist, would be barely imaginable, almost certainly miserable and undoubtedly unresponsive to moral suasion.

If, as I have been arguing, moral reasons add nothing substantial to the reasons we already have, it follows that removing the moral veneer from our repertoire of reasons removes only an illusion All our existing natural reasons are still there.

If that moral layer is mythical, as I have been arguing, then any added weight that might accrue to some of my reasons as a result of fallacious double counting is liable to lead you astray. After you discard morality, most of your reasons may remain the same, but you will have removed the distortions that morality imposed on their relative weights.

HOW REASONS ARE FUNNELLED INTO DECISIONS

In the remainder of this chapter, I want to say more about the way in which reasons relate to the actions they explain or justify. There is much debate in the professional literature about the relation between values, reasons and emotions. Some claim that reasons can only be derived from values; others argue for the reverse. Some theories regard emotions as perceptions of value; others, such as the Projectivism discussed in Chapter 3, regard values as projections from emotional responses. The advocates for competing views on these matters all make sense of the evidence, while differing mainly on which they regard as more central, That makes the disputes rather less momentous than the fervent debates they arouse might lead us to expect. Without intervening in those debates, let me say a little more about the projectivist and Bayesian perspective on reasons I have sketched.

At any given moment calling for a decision, the black box that processes all our reasons must somehow produce a binary choice: either the action is undertaken or it is not. The inaccessibility of that causal process locates the alchemy of reasons firmly in the intuitive system S1, even when, on the face of it, an agent is adducing Abeliefs as their explicit reasons. We can think of wants and desires of every kind as regimented into a single scale, for which we can borrow the term util from consequentialists. By assigning to each outcome a measure of desirability and a specific subjective probability, even the most disparate considerations are forced into comparability. The different reasons at play can then be thought of as represented by mathematical tensors. When added together, these tensors issue in a decision. In this regard, the Bayesian account of reasons provides a single scale, applicable to any conceivable goal, value or object of desire in the broadest possible sense.

The process just described, by which Bayesian reasons (sets of desirabilities and subjective probabilities) are marshalled into a single decision, is a causal one. Here, utils, in contrast with the use made of them by consequentialists, are not given any normative role. The Bayesian perspective is applicable to other animals as well as people. Figuring out the exact mechanisms involved is the stuff of psychological and brain science, but science has no interest in judging the process itself in terms of normative morality. It makes no claim about what an agent *ought* to be doing. Even when it is able to conclude that a certain decision was rational or irrational on a particular occasion—something that, as I have argued, can result only from comparing different things that agents *say* about their actions, not from the observed nature of those actions themselves—science would be committing the naturalistic fallacy if it were to infer that the agent *should* or *should not* have acted accordingly (see Box #1 in Chapter 1). If some values or wants turn out to be incommensurable after all, then there are decisions the rationality of which cannot be determined. In such cases, even the simple conditional imperative *If your goal is to achieve the best outcome of any action under present circumstances, then do X* cannot be obeyed: for there is then simply no such thing as a best outcome.

Yet, as we saw in Chapter 4, moral theories work hard to show that there is an answer to every moral question. Notably, both Kant and John Stuart Mill were inclined to deny that any situation, when analysed in depth, could constitute a genuinely insoluble moral dilemma. In such a true moral dilemma, every available option would entail doing something that is morally wrong, as in the notorious case of Sophie's choice in William Styron's novel (Styron, 1980).

For Kant, given his principle that a good will is the only thing good 'without limitation', what the good will prescribes cannot be wrong even though what it does may have bad consequences. For Utilitarian Theory, the funnelling of every possible experience into a single dimension of utility is a normative one: it is about justification, not explanation. Any experience can contribute to happiness or unhappiness, and whether it is construed in hedonic or eudaimonic terms, that contribution must be measured in utils. That manoeuvre is essential to making sense of the Principle of Utility. If there is no rational way of calculating and comparing the value in utils of different goals and values, then the Principle of Utility is literally impossible to follow. The apparent incommensurability of some of the reasons involved therefore becomes a problem for Utilitarianism.

For Bayesian Theory, by contrast, though it uses some of the same terms and calculations, justification is not in question. Every deliberation funnels continuous quantities into a binary choice: act or refrain. Some steps in the process may be merely random, but that is not a problem because normativity doesn't come into it. Randomness is ubiquitous in life, but only the moralist deplores it—because it robs morality of its grip.

What is required for R to be 'the reason' to do A

On the basis of what I have said so far, I can now clarify what it means to say that reasons are natural facts rather than normative oughts.

As we saw, we can always extract the natural fact referred to by a thick concept, disentangling it from any normative connotation that its expression might carry. The kind of natural facts in question include that the subject has a certain want, and what is expressed by the relevant conditional statements about expected outcomes. Reasons to act are sets of natural facts. We can deliberate, reconsider, take advice, exhort or be exhorted, without any need for an additional layer of moral appraisal.

Yet, you might ask, are there not normative oughts in a non-moral sense? It may appear that some practical imperatives are inherently normative without being moral. 'Take healthy nourishment', for example. Do we then not need some concept of irreducible normativity even if we are amoralist?

The answer is that moral normativity is unique because it alone issues *categorical* imperatives, which, as we saw, are unconditional and universal. Some practical precepts may appear to be normative in an equally universal yet non-moral sense, but that is only because the antecedent of the relevant hypotheticals is assumed to apply to every human being. 'Take healthy nourishment' is the consequent of a hypothetical that begins 'If you want to stay alive . . . '. As we saw, however, such claims of universality for the antecedent are factually mistaken. Some may insist that 'normativity' is involved in the mere process of acting for reasons, on the ground that reasons are grounds for judgments of what we 'should' do in a non-moral sense. But that sense is a weak one, committing one neither to categoricity nor to universality. Only morality need stake a claim to normativity in the strong sense that includes those features.

CONCLUSION: THE FALLACY OF DOUBLE COUNTING

Formulated in terms of reasons, then, morality intrudes into our deliberations and evaluations by way of the claim that some reasons are privileged. Those reasons, just by virtue of that label, acquire a special capacity to trump those that lack it. They do so in virtue of possessing inherent normativity. But normativity, I have argued, is not required for practical reasons to exist and to be acted on. The factual, natural situation that constitutes a practical reason requires no supplementary normative contribution from an additional *moral* reason. That is just as well, since there is no such thing as moral normativity. Any normativity that might seem to remain reflects merely the fact that certain natural facts provide a natural reason, in accordance with hypothetical truths about an action's consequences, for an agent with a certain configuration of wants to perform a given action.

Let me illustrate that with one more example. For greater generality, let us take one that happens to work even if you are not a human. You can be an ape or even a rat. Suppose you notice that whenever you pull a lever which delivers you some treat, you also cause another sentient being to undergo a painful electric shock. There is ample evidence that, in most cases, *that factual observation* will trigger a desire to refrain from pulling the lever despite its resulting in a pleasurable experience (Hernandez-Lallement et al., 2020). That provides you with a reason to refrain from pulling the lever. That reason will consist exclusively of natural facts, among which, of course, will be your own desires.

Now consider the move made by the moralist. The moralist regards *You ought not to pull the lever* as the application of a moral rule that says, *You ought not to cause gratuitous pain*. There are two ways, as we saw, in which we can rephrase this: we could say that the moralist has given us a second reason for not pulling the lever, so that where you originally had one reason to refrain from doing so, you now have two. Or we could say that your original reason has acquired a special label that confers on it dominance over other reasons. In the pages above, I have mentioned both construals, but I have argued that in both cases we still have one reason. Since moral reasons supervene on natural reasons, the latter are sufficient for the former. Both construals amount to taking one reason and counting it twice over, which may result in an unwarranted change in your reasons' relative weights.

What I have just written assumes that the agent, ape, rat or human, did have an (internal, that is, psychologically motivating) reason not to cause pain. What if they do not, because they simply don't care?

Setting aside for the moment the question of whether rats and apes have a morality in the human sense (though I shall be addressing the issue in Chapter 8), let us return to our sadistic tattoo artist.

Either they know they are inflicting pain, and view that as a reason to refrain, or they do not—whether out of ignorance or indifference. If they do regard it as a reason to refrain, they don't need the supplementary moral reason. If they do not, then by all means do try pressing that moral reason on them: tell them that the gratuitous infliction of pain violates a moral rule. Surely, however, it would be idle to expect a sadistic agent, previously undeterred by the pain they are inflicting, suddenly to be moved when told that inflicting pain was immoral. Why should one who is indifferent to others' pain be moved when told it is immoral? The same will hold, of course, when morality requires doing 'good' rather than refraining from 'bad': if you are unmoved by the thought of making someone happier, you are unlikely to be swayed by the thought that morality requires it.

To sum up. I have argued that the supervenience of moral reasons on natural reasons amounts to counting certain reasons twice over. The moralist claims that the agent considering an action that will cause harm has not just one but two reasons to refrain. To the first, which is that it would cause harm, morality adds a second, namely that doing so would be immoral. That moral reason, it seems, is at once both identical to the factual reason on which it supervenes, and also different from it: for only the moral reason is inherently normative. It's a mystery, like the Holy Trinity. And although in this case it's only a duality, it's no less mysterious for that. Mysteries are better shunned: they are usually scams.

7

Metaphysics is the finding of bad reasons for what we believe upon instinct.

F. H. Bradley

As we saw in Chapter 1, what *Humans are rational animals* actually means is that humans alone can be irrational. Other living things, canny though they may be, do not explicitly deliberate or contradict themselves: only *rational animals* do that. In us, the capacity for speech has enabled the development of the Analytic System S2, which has come to complement the already stunningly sophisticated Intuitive System S1. The Analytic system formulates explicit inferences. Some of those come in the form of practical reasoning, which justifies actions with reasons incorporating Abeliefs.

Since Abeliefs are what we generally refer to when we say that someone knows p or believes p without qualification, they might be thought to be subject to different standards of rationality, namely 'epistemic' rather than practical rationality. That view might be motivated by the appearance of conflict between the two, arising when a state of belief may affect the agent independently of the belief's truth value. The most notorious example of such a clash between epistemic and practical reason is known as Pascal's wager. Blaise Pascal (1623–1662), a gifted mathematician and a

DOI: 10.4324/9781003278252-7

passionate Christian apologist, argued that even if the likelihood of God's existence is infinitesimal, and the sacrifices demanded by a Christian life painfully onerous, it would be rational to believe in God and submit to the rigours of his commands. Anticipating Bayesian Decision Theory (see Box #3 in Chapter 4), he argued that the possibility of infinite bliss or infinite torture in hell, however improbable, would outweigh whatever positive or negative value might attach to a finite life. He concluded that even if believing (or disbelieving) in God affords only a tiny chance of getting heaven (or hell), belief is the better option.

Pascal's wager has not made many converts—to his argument or his faith. We needn't dwell on the objections it has faced. What is pertinent in the present context is that it ignores the distinction between theoretical and practical rationality. It does this by treating values that have nothing to do with truth—hell's torment, heaven's bliss—as relevant to the rationality of belief. Such practical consequences of believing are beside the point *if you want to believe only what is true*. That the state of believing itself is comforting or depressing, rewarded or punished, is irrelevant to its truth. Indeed, the conflation of practical interests with the inherent aim of belief is known as wishful thinking, which is generally viewed as a poor guide to life.

Nevertheless, some thinkers, from Protagoras in Ancient Greece to William James (1842–1910), have held that truth is important only because it is useful (*Chignell, 2018). In order to act effectively, an agent needs to have true beliefs about relevant facts, but useless truths are just that—useless.

In fact, the clash between theoretical Reason and practical Reason is more apparent than real. The goals of purely theoretical inquiry are 'epistemic' ones, but they are still goals, of which the two principal ones are to Abelieve truths and not to Abelieve falsehoods. Theoretical reason, then, might be regarded as just one kind of practical reason. For our purpose, which is to assess the bearing of reasons on moral responsibility, an Abelief that p is simply a commitment to the intention to treat p as true. In the words of the philosopher of science Bas van Fraassen: 'if I express my opinion, I invite the world to rely on my integrity and to infer from this what advice to myself and anyone else in like circumstances . . . I would presently consider the best' (van Fraassen, 1984, 255).

In the context of reason-giving, that means using it as an unquestioned premise in arguments for conclusions either theoretical or practical. If we specify the goal of a deliberation as epistemic—that is, that the utils to be maximised in this context are just those entailed by the goal of Abelief—then the conflict between theoretical and practical reason disappears.

Regardless of the kind of ends pursued, the core idea of rationality is simple. At the most general level, rationality is a measure of efficiency of means to ends. If your aim is practical, your means are rational if they are the most likely to achieve it (other things being equal). If your aim is to believe only what is true, perhaps in order to formulate an Abelief as an explicit reason, other goals are set aside. But with that limitation, it can be viewed as just another practical decision.

However, situations in which only truth matters are rare: the truth matters to different degrees in different contexts. And our Pbeliefs concerning the circumstances of a decision will affect the range of propositions to which we grant the status of Abelief.

Every living thing acts on reasons, if those are understood in Bayesian terms. But only 'rational animals' give reasons, that

Why It's OK to Be Amoral

is, make them explicit as Abeliefs, which might come up for judgment by others (notably the Morality Police). A reason given may be rejected, contested or at least questioned. By contrast, while animals without language can undoubtedly encounter conflicts, in the sense of having incompatible goals or competing for some resource, they cannot question one another's motives or the validity of their reasons. Only language makes that possible. So it is because of language that we are rational animals, in the categorial sense of that term in which I have been using it. That sense implies, as I have stressed, that we are ever at risk of being irrational, or seeming so to others, on the basis of things we say about what we want or believe.

And that, in short, is what threatens to make moralists of us all. For once we are in the business of giving and demanding reasons, every answer to a why-question is liable to spur further reasoning about the proposed justifications on offer, sparking debate and further why-questions. That begins, as every impatient parent knows, with a child's acquisition of language. Philosophers in general, viewed in this perspective, are suffering from intellectual neoteny—the disproportionate length of infancy characteristic of our species. Philosophers, like children, can never stop asking why. What distinguishes the moral philosophers' why-questions is that the kinds of reasons they are asking for are unlike those sought by scientists. Moralists or agents preoccupied with morality are looking not for mere explanations, but for justifications—for the kinds of explanations that show the agent did what they morally ought.

As we have seen, a common strategy for climbing up a chain of reasons is to bring your original reason under the umbrella of a more general one. Logically, however, a general statement is always more doubtful than any of its instances: that *these* swans are white doesn't prove *no* swans are black. How is it reasonable to ground a claim on another less probable one?

The response of moral theorists is to look for a foundational principle so irrefutably obvious as to warrant the certainty of any proposition it entails. The Principle of Utility and the Categorical Imperative have been prime candidates. Those principles, however, generate mutually conflicting verdicts. And since they are basic, there is no *further* principle, no firmer common ground, on the basis of which the disagreement between them can be resolved.

In a typical deliberation, whether moral or merely prudential, intuitions about specific cases may be confronted with intuitions about more general principles. You might want to feed a hungry pigeon, but also reflect that in general feeding hungry pigeons is liable to result in being swarmed with more hungry pigeons, a general condition that you do not want. You will then look for a 'reflective equilibrium', by adjusting either your general or your particular wants, in order to bring them as much as possible into harmony. Sometimes, you will modify your preference in the specific case in the light of the more general principle. But at other times the quest for reflective equilibrium will redirect your attention to intuitions about specific cases (such as the plight of this particular pigeon), of which you may feel more confident than you are of the general principle. In many cases, you will be right in regarding your specific intuitions as more reliable than those concerning foundational absolutes, for it is a logical truth that the probability of a more general statement is always lower than that of any of its instances.

Besides, those particular intuitions are likely to be the original reasons you were aware of, before the moralist came in to dictate general rules. Hence the detour via foundations seems to demand that we justify the more plausible by the more dubious, *obscurum per obscurius*—the obscure by the more obscure.

Or so I shall be arguing in this chapter.

WHICH JUSTIFICATION LADDER
SHALL YOU SCRAMBLE UP?

In Chapters 2 and 3, we surveyed a number of approaches to the justification of reasons. Unsurprisingly, each one of these proposals confronted a number of objections. Let me briefly recall the main ones.

Divine Command Theory requires you to make a truly vertiginous number of existential choices. If you conservatively assume some ten thousand sects to choose from, you must, if you are to be conscientious, make about 50 million pairwise comparisons. That seems discouraging.

In practice, of course, you seldom make any choice at all. You were brought up in some particular place at some particular time, and you will have been told what to believe before you ever become aware of alternatives. That makes the odds of being right one in ten thousand, which also seems discouraging.

If you are tempted to look to Nature, we saw that of the two ways that has been tried, neither succeeds. The Natural Law tradition requires you both to understand what actually happens in Nature and, more implausibly, to have some means of knowing what Nature really *intended* to happen. But Nature intends nothing. Alternatively, if you are to take Nature as it is as your guide to what is right, the cruel debaucheries of the Marquis de Sade have as good a claim as any other pursuits to Nature's Seal of Approval. That is not an implication that moralists will welcome.

In sum, neither Divine Command Theory nor conformity with Nature can provide the universal principle required. Unsurprisingly, the appeal to the Justifier that needs no justification echoes the theologian's call for an Uncaused Cause. In traditional theology, the existence of an Uncaused Cause is inferred from a premise that it seems to contradict, which is that nothing can exist without a cause. Similarly, the inference to a First Principle that needs no justification contradicts its own premise, which is that every rule stands in need of justification.

ENTER THE PHILOSOPHERS

Understandably, therefore, philosophers have sought a foundational principle so compelling that no one, regardless of cultural background, can fail to assent to it. Its universality is essential, inasmuch as moralists and moral philosophers agree, as we have seen, that moral relativism must be incoherent. Utilitarianism, Kantian Deontology and Contractarianism have been the most widely influential of those attempts. Each one posits one or more reasons that you can't reject. The function of those ultimate reasons is to identify the supreme why-stopper, the one that either trumps or justifies all others.

For Utilitarianism, the putatively undeniable claim is that pleasure, pain, happiness and unhappiness, appropriately assessed and comprehensively calculated, leave no room for further justification. In Kantian Deontology, the core strategy seems even more unanswerable, since it appeals to the supposed conceptual necessity of the inference sequence from doing something to being an agent, to being rational, to being bound by a self-legislated moral law.

Let us look a little closer at how this works out for each of the two main contestants for ethical supremacy: Utilitarianism Consequentialism and Kantian Deontology.

Why no conversions?

I begin by noting that while undergraduates in an introductory philosophy class might well be asked to contrast Kantian Deontology with Utilitarianism, the gulf is so wide that most professional philosophers tend to stay in one camp or the other. If you scan the Tables of Contents of professional journals, you will see countless articles developing detailed arguments about specific issues arising within one or the other of those traditions. But it would be too much for either to undertake refuting the other as a whole. Each is, in its own way, literally irrefutable.

Furthermore, while philosophical practitioners take pride in following where the argument leads, and changing their minds when they find they have been led astray, no philosopher that I know has been persuaded by honest debate to switch their allegiance from Utilitarianism to Kantian Deontology or vice versa. The spirit of those approaches is so different that doing so would resemble a religious conversion more than a change of mind resulting from rational persuasion.

In religion, conversions are rare. They come to our attention precisely because their rarity matches their apparent randomness. They seem inexplicable because disinterested observers find it hard to make sense of whatever the convert regarded as decisive. I am not speaking, obviously, of conversions required of a prospective spouse to placate prospective in-laws. I have in mind the type of story still referred to as a 'Road to Damascus' event.

On the original Road to Damascus, Saul, a fanatical persecutor of Christians, was struck by lightning. That, after three days of blindness, transformed him into an equally fanatical follower of Jesus Christ. Saul, we are told in chapter 9 of the *Acts of the Apostles*, felt his sight restored, got up and was baptised. And that was that. Saul became Paul, who with unchanging zeal, having simply switched sides, inspired some of the most intolerant rules and ruthless persecutions imposed by Christians on fellow Christians and others.

What is remarkable about that conversion, and is equally striking in other conversions such as those of Cardinal Newman (1801–1890) or Ronnie Knox (the witty Catholic convert whose limericks we sampled in Chapter 3) is that their characters or temperaments remain unchanged, while the reasons they adduced for their doctrinal reversal seem stunningly feeble.

In that respect, Utilitarianism and Kantian Deontology are not unlike religious sects. If philosophical conversions are equally rare, it may be due to the seldom acknowledged role played by character and intellectual temperament in determining philosophical preferences.[1]

That is not to say that either side is in want of formidable arguments. It's rather that each team is better at offence than defence. Each sees the other's defects while they struggle in sophisticated ways to evade or deny their own.

In a moment, I shall give some illustrations of these very general arguments. But first, a reminder of the ways in which each of the two competing systems is led to propose, at the end of any series of why-questions, a fundamental principle from which the justification of all other principles is supposed to follow logically.

Why-stopping: Pleasures and pains or logic

Utilitarianism's appeal to the why-stopping power of happiness, unhappiness, pleasure and pain is persuasive to common sense. Yet some have found ways to disagree. J. S. Mill himself contended with the objection that a preoccupation with pleasure was degrading and bestial. Some religious thinkers have even found positive value in pain. Witness, for example, Pope John Paul's Apostolic Letter *Salvifici Doloris* ('On the Salvific Power of Suffering'), which extols suffering as something to be welcomed in itself: 'Assuming . . . that throughout his earthly life man walks in one manner or another on the long path of suffering', John Paul writes, 'suffering seems to belong to man's transcendence: it is one of those points in which man is in a certain sense "destined" to go beyond himself, and he is called to this in a mysterious way' (John Paul II, 1984).

John Paul's Apostolic Letter may not convince you that suffering in itself can ever be desirable, but it does show that not everyone shares the ultimate premise on which Utilitarianism rests.

By contrast, Kantian Deontology's fundamental principle is supposed to be intelligible based on reason alone. But while we expect unanimous verdicts among those competent to judge in logic and mathematics, the concept of conceptual necessity is almost as much disputed as that of morality. (*Kment, 2021). Every step in the Kantian syllogism is contested. First, that one has done something intentionally does not logically entail that one is a rational agent in the requisite sense. The next step asserts or takes for granted that any rational agent is 'bound' by the Categorical Imperative. The relevant sense of 'binding' involved is metaphorical and, given how easily those supposed bonds are broken, remains particularly hard to explicate.

So here again, when engaged in a deliberation requiring you to determine what you should regard yourself as 'bound' to, there is little you can turn to beside commonsense intuitions.

That is not to say that each system cannot summon plausible intuitions targeting the other. Each system can score some obvious points.

Against Kantian Deontology

Utilitarians, for one, can charge Kantian Deontology with failure to take account of the consequences of actions, in ways that can seem callous and unfeeling. Because Kantian Deontology focuses on the intentions and moral duties associated with an action, it appears entitled to disregard its consequences. *Fiat justitia, ruat caelum* sums it up: Let justice be done, though the heavens fall. While utilitarians do sometimes rely on rules, as we saw in Chapter 4, these are mere shortcuts intended for use when the calculation of consequences is particularly unfeasible. A rule utilitarian would be expected to switch to act Utilitarianism in the face of an obviously urgent threat. The Categorical Imperative precludes such flexibility.

Kantian deontologists are also vulnerable to the complaint that the Categorical Imperative gives little practical guidance. Insofar as it is based on the idea of dignity, it struggles to come up with a definition of that elusive concept. Dignity is all too close in its meaning and associations to the notion of honour, which is notoriously dependent on the local culture in which it is invoked.

Furthermore, the test of universalisability requires us to identify what Kant calls the 'maxim' of any action, but it is hard to see how the maxim of an action differs from what the agent claims their intention to be. Am I telling a lie, which the Categorical Imperative forbids? Or am I attempting to save an innocent life, which must surely be at least permissible?

Any chain of why-questions can be paired with a parallel chain of by-questions, unpacking an intention as that by which a further goal is to be achieved. When you open the fridge door, so as to get some cheese, so as to make a sandwich, you are engaged in making a sandwich, by getting some cheese, by opening the fridge door. Which is the 'maxim' of your action? Which, in more familiar terms, is your real point and intent? To answer that question is an exercise in casuistry, a fun game that some contemporary Kantians might be eager to play. But it remains difficult to see how the Categorical Imperative can be of much use to an ordinary person trying to make a moral choice.

Against Utilitarianism

From the Kantian point of view, Utilitarianism also provides some easy targets. Kantians emphasise the inherent worth of each individual. They can complain that focusing on maximising overall happiness encourages the neglect of individual rights and dignity. Just as the anecdote of the fatally truthful friend provides a key gotcha against Kantians, there is a key gotcha against Utilitarianism. It features a standard vignette in which the pursuit of maximum happiness for the greatest number requires the enslavement of one innocent.

Again, utilitarians have ad hoc ways of parrying that criticism, if only by adding an additional constraint. One can just supplement the maximising of happiness by requiring it to be justly distributed. That strategy brings some additional challenges, however. For principles of justice involve placeholders that need to be filled. The specific content that should fill those slots varies from one culture to another. The basic principle of justice is that each should get what they deserve, but does that depend on their rank? their caste? their effort? their market clout? their need? their sex or gender? or even their species? For each of these, some distinct status has been advocated or allocated by some political or social doctrine at some place or time. How to fill the placeholder is something that utilitarians can address by the usual methods, combining plausible speculation with an exaggerated appearance of precision. From the point of view of a typical WEIRD citizen, it seems obvious enough that respecting caste or rank or market clout could not guarantee the maximisation of happiness. The actual calculations involved, however, are likely to be driven by the results desired a priori. Plausible statistics and psychological generalisations will be invented, nicely reverse-engineered to produce the results favoured by those who adduce them.

Utilitarians can concede that calculating consequences is daunting indeed, but insist that ignoring consequences altogether is worse. But how distant are the consequences worth computing? The 'butterfly effect' dramatises the futility of long-term predictions. As Maynard Keynes has quipped, in the long term we shall all be dead.

Extreme longtermism

But what about the longish term, when we are all dead but distant descendants are still alive? Should we be trying to plan for a million years hence?

An influential group of philosophers, notably William MacAskill, have advocated thinking of the long term as the average life of a species. That means considering the interests of all descendants of currently living humans for the next million years. From that perspective, MacAskill writes:

> morality, at its core, is about putting ourselves in others' shoes and treating their interests as we do our own. When we do this at the full scale of human history, the future—where almost everyone lives and where almost all potential for joy and misery lies—comes to the fore.
> (MacAskilll, 2022)

Extreme longtermists have persuaded some influential billionaires (or ex-billionaires such as the now convicted fraudster Sam Bankman-Fried) that their philanthropy should prioritise our species' survival a million years from now. More predictable goals in the foreseeable future, such as reversing climate change or eliminating malaria, come far behind. For if our species does survive, there will be trillions or quadrillions whose collective amount of happiness will swamp that of the mere billions alive in the next century or two. That will be so even if the latter are left miserable, and even if the average happiness of each of those quadrillion unborn humans barely manages to break even. That implies that longtermists don't have to rely on their oddly confident expectation that the humans of a million years hence will have established utopian paradises all over the galaxy (Torres, 2022).

Two aspects of this longtermism seem especially preposterous—in a very literal meaning of that word, putting first things last. One, of which I've already said enough, is the very idea that we could hazard any prediction about consequences a hundred years hence, let alone a million. A more subtle issue concerns the unargued assumption that the extinction of the human race itself would be a Bad Thing. While questioning that assumption might seem shocking, it may be less so when we look at the two separate claims it comprises. The first is that non-existent people have interests, which we have a moral obligation to consider. The second is that those interests include being born rather than not.

Here is how the first of those propositions might be questioned. It is clearly true of many people that they care about some unborn persons, the possibility of whose existence is more or less vividly envisaged. You might care about your grandchildren, or the future fans of your masterpiece. But it isn't obvious that anyone should care, morally or sentimentally, about humans or posthumans who might exist a hundred thousand years from now. To fathom the absurdity of longtermism, it is enough to reflect that no specific prediction of anything that far in the future is probable enough to justify anything at all.

Furthermore, anything we do that alters the course of future history in even minor ways will likely prevent some persons from ever existing. That follows from the fact that every human being is the unique product of one spermatozoon among millions produced in a single ejaculation, in conjunction with one ovum from among many hundred thousand oocytes lying in wait in a female's ovaries. Any event that results in a change in the timing of a copulation by even a few seconds will cause a different spermatozoon to be involved. If a baby is born, it will not be the one that would have existed were it not for that small change in timing. It can therefore be said that anything you do to improve the lives of future persons will actually prevent some of those future persons from ever existing. I leave it to moralists, especially those who deem themselves 'pro-life', to judge whether such an action is morally acceptable. Can you be deemed to increase the happiness of any persons, when what you do actually ensures that *those very future persons* will never be born?

Your opinion on this somewhat abstruse question will in part depend on your verdict on the second of the two propositions above: that it is better to be born than not. That assumption has indeed been challenged, not only by the author of *Ecclesiastes* (4:3) and by Sophocles' Oedipus, but by a respected contemporary philosopher. David Benatar has invoked an asymmetry between the goodness of pleasure or happiness and the badness of pain or suffering. The asymmetry results from taking the absence of pleasure as merely neutral, while the absence of pain is positively good. Every life contains, at best, both pleasure and pain. But for the unborn, the absence of pain is a positive good while the absence of pleasure is not an evil. In the balance, then, not being born is better than being born, for it alone has some good and no bad (Benatar, 2006).

Once again, the point is not that Benatar's argument is decisive. On the contrary: there is really nothing except unaided off-the-top-of-your-head intuition to justify any specific assignment of value to the absence of pain in an unborn being, or to compare that with the value of existence in the lifetime of one who gets to draw a breath. There is obviously no conceivable way in which such assignments could be justified. The point is only to exhibit how dubious are the arbitrary assumptions on which the longtermist version of Consequentialism is based.

The Kingdom of Ends

Since the deontologist is not primarily concerned with consequences, they can evade the need to pronounce on duties stemming from what might happen a million years from now. They can still, however, appeal to non-existent entities. These are the denizens of the Kingdom of Ends, each of whom respects every other agent, and never uses them solely as a means to their own selfish ends.

Equipped with that concept, Kantians can plausibly defy the consequentialist to deny that the happiness of all, in such an ideal community, is bound to be greater than in a world in which every agent attempts to calculate consequences on the basis of bare intuitions. That hypothetical conclusion seems as plausible a consequentialist calculation as any adduced by the utilitarian.

Even that much might be contested, however. The Kingdom of Ends, like most philosophers' utopias, is hopelessly underdescribed. From the point of view of what passed for science fiction just a few decades ago, you already live in Utopia. You can read almost any book or listen to almost any music at the touch of a few buttons. By speaking aloud next to a robot assistant the size of a cigarette case, you can instantaneously obtain information that would have once required weeks of trudging through libraries. You can see and talk to people around the world at no cost. All of this might have been imagined, but was hardly predicted a few decades ago when Thomas Watson, head of IBM, opined that the world would only ever need five computers. Neither could you have imagined unintended consequences, such as the chaos and mental anguish inflicted by some of those very wonders, or the impoverishment of the artists and creators whose work you can now so easily enjoy.

And yet you still belong in a world where you can understand Thucydides or Shakespeare. Technology has changed us in unpredictable ways, but not as much as would be needed to feel at home into the Kingdom of Ends. That realm, I surmise, would be stranger than any real or fictional world humans have imagined. Who knows how much of it would remain intelligible? The commonsense psychology presupposed by the entire corpus of world literature was already opaque to the denizens of Aldous Huxley's *Brave New World*. The Kingdom of Ends might make it seem not merely unrecognisable but inhuman and unappealing, like that evoked by Susan Wolf in her essay on the rebarbative prospect of living with 'moral saints' (Wolf, 2015). If you were parachuted into the Kingdom of Ends, you might not want to live there after all. If anything is certain, it is that there is just no way to tell.

THE INCOMMENSURABLE CHARACTER
OF FUNDAMENTAL PRINCIPLES

Given the highly trained ingenuity of the contestants, the sort of debate I have imagined between Utilitarianism and Kantian Deontology will not soon abate. Much the same, you may say, can be said of scientific debate about the ultimate constituents of matter or the origins of life. The difference is that for arguments advanced in the latter sort of debate there are generally recognised criteria of success and failure. Despite the fashionable preoccupation with paradigms and paradigm shifts, sometimes backed by claims of incommensurability (*Oberheim & Hoyningen-Huene, 2018), scientific methods, as distinct from scientific opinions, enjoy a relatively high level of consensus. Theories, including conceptions of paradigms and paradigm shifts, may be disputed, but standards of evidence and patterns of inference are still agreed on within any established scientific domain, and we expect disagreements about fundamental laws of nature to be resolved in time, as a result of further application of fundamental methods that remain generally agreed on.

By contrast, in the case of morality, it is precisely the fundamental methods that are at issue. Even when they agree on some particular moral verdict, the disagreement about how to arrive at that verdict undermines it, by suggesting that it rests on doubtful foundations. The absence of any higher-order principles to which both sides can appeal makes both subject to doubt.

To illustrate this, imagine that you are a Martian immigrant who has just joined an Earthling society. You are trying to understand moral systems with a view to subscribing to the best. You have normal humanlike intuitions about the practical conditionals that you encounter in your life among humans. Now suppose that you seek to support your decisions with more basic reasons. You are presented with chains of justification that snake up towards increasingly general foundational principles. One of those chains leads to the Principle of Utility, while the other leads to the Categorical Imperative. You will then be struck by the oddity of your situation. You have committed yourself to rational agency. That means, in part, that for any decision you make you will require a reason that you can endorse. You will endorse no reason unless you feel you can justify it. And you have reached the end of the best chain of reasoning you can devise.

The problem is that there is no single best chain. The process can take you in at least two different directions. When you reach the end of each line of justification, you find that each is supported by some intuitions, and each faces weighty objections. As a result, you may feel less confident now about either than you felt about the original intuitions for which you sought justification. Since no arbitration procedure is trusted by both sides, you would be well advised to give up on both, and fall back on the original natural reasons you sought to justify.

It is unsurprising, then, that ethical theorists spend an enormous amount of time debating minute points of detail, either taking for granted the validity of one or the other of those major frameworks or ignoring the question of foundations altogether.

For illustration, sample the Tables of Contents of professional journals. In a recent issue of the most important journal in ethics, we find, for example, a paper on the extent of harm one is morally entitled to cause in self-defence; a discussion of the relative moral worth of lying and misleading; an argument against a utopian prescription that would require every child to be parented by the best available parent. (*The best parent? Really?*) In my library catalogue, I find books discussing this or that duty: *Is there a duty to die? Is there a duty to obey the law? Is whistleblowing a duty? Is there duty of procreation? Or a moral duty to refrain from procreating?*

These questions illustrate the petty concern with bringing everything and everyone under the whip of moral judgment, as I illustrated in Chapter 4. Any intelligent person who is not a doctoral candidate in philosophy, or competing for a job teaching philosophy, will recognise the shocking proportion of journal articles that focus either on questions so minute as to be nugatory, or so momentous as to admit only the sorts of grand but arbitrary intuitions surveyed in the last few pages. In the first class, I place the question of devising an algorithm to evaluate the relative moral worth of supererogatory acts (those that systems of morality require in unspecified degree, such as donations to charity). In the second, I place (real) discussions of whether to have children, or whether you have a duty to love them if you do. The last example seems especially futile: for if philosophy persuades you that you do have such a duty, how will that help you if you don't love your child? You might already—for many good reasons—*want* to love the child, and be doing all you can to bond with it. If so, thinking of it as a duty will only make you feel guilty without making it easier to succeed. Or else you may simply not care about it, in which case, once again, calling it a moral duty is unlikely to move you.

BAD MORALITIES

When different societies have conflicting interests, they can negotiate to avoid going to war. But when they disagree about moral values, there may be no common ground on which to negotiate or compromise. Disagreement becomes a 'clash of civilisations', in which each is committed to 'fundamental', non-negotiable principles. From inside any one such system, competing systems are simply evil.

I have already mentioned the moral fervour displayed by Heinrich Himmler, the architect of Nazi death camps, and his pride in his ability to overcome the distress it caused him to view the killings his 'duty' required of him. Consider also the judges of the Spanish Inquisition, who, out of the purest altruistic concern for their victims' immortal souls, had them burned alive at the stake. Far from thinking of themselves as immoral, each of them regarded himself (for they were obviously only men) as guardians of a superior moral order grounded in the laws of God or Nature. Moral idealism often lies at the root of the most unspeakable crimes. From the inside, every totalising morality is equally worth dying or killing for.

As I write, Taliban moralists, no less self-righteous than Spanish inquisitors with their *autos-da-fé*, are imposing their morality not only in Afghanistan. Under different banners, they are moralising with equal fervour in those states and States where, in the name of morality, laws are enacted to crush women's autonomy, force them to give birth regardless of their will or their means, or jail them for being the helpless victims of a miscarriage. Morality in action today in America treats citizens like the denizens of Erewhon, where crime is a sickness and sickness as a crime (Butler, 1872).

But, of course, you will say, *those* modes of moralising are not *really* moral: they are evil. Their perpetrators just haven't yet been educated into the *true* morality. That is easy to understand, so long as we are able to judge them objectively, in terms of what we know is *really* right and *really* good.

But if their conviction, no less than yours, is an elaboration of dispositions to moral emotions instilled into our social species by natural selection, then we are once again at a loss for any shared higher principles to which we can appeal for arbitration. Each society has shaped the same atavistic emotions into a more or less coherent system of prohibitions and commands, endorsed without question by most members of that community. That rough local consensus among the members of any given society constitutes morality as an institution. The essence of morality as an institution lies not so much in its content as in the form of certainty and the normative passion with which it is imposed.

As such, it is not easily dismantled. But once aware of its nature, you might begin to resist the feeling of entitlement that you were brought up to take for granted. 'Our' morality will always present itself as the 'true' morality, whoever 'we' happen to be. Once you become aware of this fact, you will have taken the first step towards amoralism. As an amoralist, you can come to realise that whatever your wants are, there is no body of objective moral facts that lend them superior authority. You can come to see that even if the moral domain were to be satisfactorily demarcated, no moral reason exists except in virtue of a set of natural facts on which it supervenes. Nothing stops you from taking account of all your reasons, without needing to varnish some of them with the lacquer of morality. As I shall be suggesting in Chapter 8, these are the realisations that lie at the core of the amoralist life.

What is it like to be an amoralist?

8

I have been debunking morality on the basis of its totalising tendency, its illegitimate projection of parochial prejudice transmuted into claims of priority, the failure of its
attempt at a universally valid demarcation of its domain and
its stubborn resistance to the ideas of cultural relativity and
individual diversity. By cultural relativity, I have in mind the
way in which values of all kinds, practical, moral or aesthetic,
apparently come to be shared and shaped in vast networks
of interconnected and multidirectional causation. Since those
are not the same in all places and times, it would be unrealistic to expect people everywhere to want the same things.
Individual diversity refers not only to the fact that one human
can desire what to others is beyond imagination. It stems also,
as I argued in Chapter 5, from our defective access to an individual's causally effective motives, even in our own case, on
the basis of the reasons we avow.

As an individual attempting to decide how to conduct my
life, it would seem unreasonable to ignore the expectations
and customs of my community. But neither can I assume that
my culture has all the answers. Fortunately, no society of any

DOI: 10.4324/9781003278252-8

size can ever be totally homogeneous. Dissent, in thought if not deed, always exists. So how, if you are disenchanted with the universalist pretensions of morality, should you live?

That very question will once again raise doubts about the coherence of my argument. What can I mean by 'should' if I repudiate the distinctive moral should? I have been urging that we *should* discard our obsessive concern with absolute imperatives proclaimed from moral castles in the air. But that is no moral 'should'. We can be guided instead by ordinary practical arguments about ways or means of attaining goals we contingently choose. Plain practical reasons, expressed, as I urged, in factual or hypothetical conditionals, seem unavailable to me here. Recall that such conditionals are generally answers to *What should I do if I want X?* But when the question asked is 'How should I live?' there is no suitable conditional in sight. How should I live . . . if what? The only answer that suggests itself is *If you want to live well.* But that answer merely repeats the question, and once again we are spinning in a circle. In this chapter, I will attempt to answer a more modest if-question: *How shall I live if I want to live amorally?*

To prepare the ground for my answer, let me sketch, from an amoralist perspective, how values emerge from your wants, as I suggested a moment ago, by being both trained and modified by some sort of consilience among the members of your community.

HOW WE GET OUR VALUES

In the absence of a Platonic Idea of the Good inscribed from birth into every human brain, an infant can acquire 'values' only from the instruction and example of their caretakers. This applies equally to fashion, sport, games, etiquette, art, music and more—to moral and non-moral domains, if you still think that distinction meaningful.

Yet not every child will adopt, unmodified, the values and beliefs to which they are exposed. Individual temperament influences each child's point of equilibrium between conformity and rebellion. That balancing point is a specifically human form of the trade-off between exploitation and exploration, or imitation and innovation, on which, as we saw in Chapter 2, the survival of the species may depend. That point of balance, for any given individual, is itself shaped by culture, but not identically for all.

Below the level of fully conscious deliberate action, we have acquired all kinds of attitudes, behavioural dispositions and skills. That accounts for much of what we mean by culture. However much ink, bile and blood the word has spilled, 'culture' can be defined succinctly. In the words of Mohan Matthen: 'A culture is a body of beliefs, preferences, and behavioral dispositions—"mental attitudes," for short—that are transmitted from one individual to another within an inter-communicating network of individuals (a "community")' (Matthen, 2024, p. 39).

Matthen further distinguishes between two levels of cultural influence. At the basic level, we can remain largely unaware of our culture's distinctive and often highly parochial character. Indeed, we often assume that our own crowd's ways are natural, and so we follow them without taking note of them and to that extent may take them to be universal. But culture's more powerful binding power stems from *reflexive* domains of cultural influence. Those are constituted by beliefs and attitudes that are adopted, at least in part, to satisfy one's desire to identify with the community within which they are viewed as a mark of belonging.

Unlike the basic form of cultural influence, reflexive or culturally based attitudes are consciously adopted precisely because they are felt to mark those who share them as insiders, members of a tribe. They constitute social identities. In defining who belongs, an identity of this kind comes to serve primarily to exclude those that do not. It therefore tends to intensify and moralise the cultural characteristics most likely to strengthen tribal attitudes. As a casual scroll through social media will all too quickly illustrate, the conflicting views associated with reflexive cultural identities are typically expressed in highly moralistic terms. If your tribe is not my tribe, it is not merely different; rather, it is guilty, morally blameworthy, deserving of suppression, silencing, 'cancelling'.

Thus, while cultural differences often spur more curiosity than hostility, they tend to mutate into moralising crusades when they are construed as essential to cultural identity. Take, for example, the outrage generated periodically on the Internet by the dissemination of a regional recipe. Only unimpeachable membership of the relevant community can authorise deviations from the crusader's conception of authenticity. Traditional Spaghetti Carbonara, for example, is made with eggs, cheese, pancetta and black pepper. People have anathemised the addition of cream. Others have excoriated Sushi Rolls made with cream cheese or mayonnaise, or Gumbo that includes tomatoes.

The tone of these complaints is reminiscent of those once associated with heresies deserving of *auto-da-fé*. With comparable vehemence, accusations of 'cultural appropriation' are levelled against artists or writers who, in another age, would have been admired for their empathy with lives different from their own. Sometimes there may be reasons to object to 'cultural appropriation', when an oppressive inequality favours the borrower over the borrowed-from. But those reasons would suffice without imputing moral turpitude to those whom another culture has inspired.

Interactions between child and parent, student and teacher; social consensus and individual preferences—all these will form and re-form every individual's range of accommodation and resistance. At any time, a complex web of interactions connects intuitions, rational arguments, social and personal influences, and reappraisals, leading to fresh intuitions. As causal influences flow in all directions, patterns will form and re-form (Haidt & Björklund, 2008). A snapshot of a social group at some time will capture, for any belief, attitude, taste or behavioural disposition, a profile approximating the bell curve of a normal distribution. That profile will feature a mode, comprising a plurality of most frequent adopters, and tails, representing extremes of rejection on one side and fanatical endorsement of the other. Thus, even in the most homogeneous culture, conformity will admit of degrees, and thus provide the majority with opportunities to blame those in the minority for their failure to match the majority's moralistic expectations. If only all could be persuaded to adopt amoralism, they would live and let live, to the benefit of all.

The distribution of religious faith in North America provides a convenient illustration. Currently, the configuration is on the move, with a mode shifting slowly away from religion (Inglehart, 2020). At one tail of the curve, there are radical atheists; at the other, fanatical fundamentalists, while a plurality in between pays at least lip service to some version of faith. And the moralisers in the majority get to whip up a moral panic about how they are the victims of persecution. A similar picture reflects tastes in native or exotic cuisines, in various forms of art and styles of music, and in the specific moral attitudes that generate heated debates on social media. Some cultures have favoured tradition over innovation, to the point of dressing up any new ideas in the guise of old ones just recovered. The WEIRD culture that surrounds me in urban centres of contemporary North America lies at the opposite extreme: it prizes innovation and boasts of 'breaking things' more than any other in the past. That attitude is no doubt an inherent feature of technology in a capitalist economic system. It also applies to the arts and fashion, and perhaps even to philosophy. And certainly, also to the strength of individuals' allegiance to the different domains of morality distinguished in Chapter 4 (Haidt & Joseph, 2007).

One might speculate about the extent to which the tireless search for innovation exacerbates the excess of moral fervour I have been deploring. Many disagreements have come to seem emblematic of some major clash of civilisations, in which each side feels, irrationally, that it has everything to lose. On one side, any disruptive change is viewed as an attack on core traditional values; the other side is equally passionate in its quest to uncover and amend oppressive inequalities, racism and sexism, that are seen as blocking the very 'moral progress' which their opponents decry as moral decadence. The moral passion on both sides illustrates how moral attitudes tend to obscure the reasons that inhere in the actual situations that elicit desire or aversion.

Moral progress is obviously not something amoralists aspire to. But that should not stop you from viewing some changes favourably. There is no need to sort the different changes one approves of into moral ones and others. When people speak of moral progress, the changes they generally have in mind pertain to very broad features of social organisation on the one hand and majority attitudes to those features on the other. An amoralist can approve of or desire the abolition of slavery or the end of gender and racial discrimination as fervently as any moralist. Or, for that matter, they can resent the decline of patriarchy and the lack of respect from the lower classes to their social superiors. Those differences can be debated on their merits, without appealing to an additional layer of moralistic rhetoric or principle.

Amoralists can invoke reasons, weigh them against one another and test them for rationality and consistency. This can involve explicit argument and debate, though, as we saw in Chapter 5, much of that scrutiny may well require reaching below the threshold of consciousness. When endeavouring to make their reasons explicit, amoralists will seek a reflective equilibrium of the sort discussed in the previous chapter, both among themselves and in each individual's mind.

Now if both moralist and amoralist alike pursue a reflective equilibrium among their reasons, what difference does it make if you are an amoralist? The answer is best explained by looking at the spirit in which each one pursues reflective equilibrium. The realist about morality is seeking to weigh objectively existing values against one another. But given the failure of all arguments for the possibility of accessing any such stance-independent realm of moral truth, there can be no measure of those values other than each agent's subjective attitude: what you are weighing against one another are all wants. Given the non-existence of any moral facts, that holds for the most fervent objectivist as well as for the projectivist. They differ merely in that the former is in denial, while the projectivist lives with the knowledge that while their wants have surely been influenced by what others want, yet they are never backed by the warrant of some objective, stance-independent moral reality.

HOW SHOULD I LIVE . . . IF I AM AN AMORALIST?

Still, to one who abjures moral principles and systems, the question *How should I live?* can still make sense and poses a challenge. Is that not precisely the question that morality is designed to answer? And does not a rejection of the very category of moral judgments imply that the question makes no sense?

In response, let me remind you once again that every supposed moral reason supervenes on natural facts. Those natural facts, however, constitute reasons only in conjunction with attitudes. That is the force of the 'projectivist' view sketched in Chapter 3: the values are created—albeit through a complicated process—by our attitudes. The attitudes in question consist broadly speaking in emotions and wants. One version of Projectivism is defended by Joel Marks as *Desirism*: it is the view that what we experience as moral imperatives are just interpretations of certain sorts of desires. It encourages us to acknowledge that fact, and to strive for rationally coherent rather than 'moral' desires. (Marks, 2012, 2016.) I prefer the term *want*, as more inclusive, but the terminology isn't important. Neither is the phenomenology of the many ways in which we experience wants, from hopes to whims to lust to 'feelings of obligation'. Each kind of want is ultimately manifested in the causal role it plays in the elaboration of any decision; it is represented in the Bayesian framework as a degree of desirability

Abjuring the spurious authority of morality, therefore, in no way impedes our efforts to reflect on our reasons. An amoralist, no less than anyone else, can bring competing reasons into confrontation, carefully check the facts that constitute them and refine and clarify what they want in the light of rational deliberation. The amoralist is no less likely than the moralist to seek and promote much of what the latter profess to value—kindness, justice and equality, or the well-being of others. (They may be just a little less likely to endorse authoritarian fascism.) The difference is that as an amoralist you will not seek to justify prioritising one set of 'moral' reasons over others, practical, prudential or aesthetic. Indeed, you can become more sensitive to the multifarious diversity of what you care about, without attempting to force every choice into a Procrustean system of duties, prohibitions and permissions. To the extent that your emotional nature allows, you can replace self-undermining guilt with more dispassionate assessments of the rationality of your past behaviour, and shape your future in the light of everything you care about. You can also hope to tame or even altogether give up the dubious pleasures of superiority that come from blaming and punishing others.

ANIMAL MORALITY?

If we take seriously the suggestion that our inclination to moralise is something we might 'tame', we might be willing to ask whether morality might actually be a kind of atavistic trait, something like the savage instincts of wolves that domestication has overcome in dogs. If that seems preposterous, it is because it has long been assumed that our capacity for morality represents the highest achievement of human mentality. Darwin himself held that 'of all the differences between man and the lower animals the moral sense or conscience is by far the most important' (Ayala, 2010). And we have seen how, for Kant as well as for Hobbes, though in very different ways, morality requires a capacity for deliberation, explicit argument and debate, of the sort associated with System 2 (see Box #4 in Chapter 5).

Recent work on animal mentality, however, has tended to narrow the gap between humans and non-language-speaking animals from both sides. Attributions of purposes, intentions and planning to non-human animals are no longer derided as anthropomorphism (Andrews, 2020). Conversely, we have come to recognise that not all our own intelligent thinking requires the use of language. As we saw in Chapter 5, the Intuitive System S1 is responsible for most of our intelligent choices without the need for explicit deliberation. In short, other animals are more like us than we used to think, and we are more like them. Perhaps, then, it is time to question the confidence with which philosophers have taken our species superiority for granted. Should we really accept the dogma that our disposition to moralism is the supreme proof of our species' transcendence of mere animal nature? Or might it make more sense, on the contrary, to view it as a kind of atavism or vestigial trait, one of the legacies of evolution that we might strive to overcome?

To see why this idea might not be as implausible as might first appear, recall that the noncognitivist views of morality discussed in Chapter 3 stressed the essential role played by emotional dispositions. As discussed in that chapter, the moral emotions associated with the principal domains of morality are present in other animals. Those include, notably, the negative emotion elicited by causing harm, the tendency to defer to hierarchy and the impulse to favour members of our own tribe. If, then, morality is driven by emotions, and moral emotions are shared with other animals, morality cannot plausibly be seen as a capability that distinguishes us from other animals and shows us to be superior.

Furthermore, emotions, however much they have been elaborated and refined by rational deliberation, cannot help but retain aspects of their evolutionary origins. We saw in Chapter 2 that what has been bequeathed us by natural selection cannot be counted on to benefit us even if it consists in traits that were originally adaptive. That applies to any characteristics of our emotions if they are likely to have been honed by natural selection in the distant past. To illustrate this, consider what might be called McDonald emotions.

The success of McDonald's menus is due to the fact that most of what they serve is particularly rich in sugar, fat and salt. All three are nutritional elements that would have been at a premium at some stage in our evolutionary past, as both essential to survival and sometimes difficult to secure. In present-day North America, by contrast, most diets contain all three in unhealthy abundance. We crave foods rich in those ingredients even when we no longer need them.

Similarly, the emotions that are crucial to the formation of early societies, while they undoubtedly include compassionate feelings of concern for members of one's own tribe, also favour ruthless hostility to outsiders. Natural selection may also have promoted possessive jealousy and lethal rage, the effects of which are much different when agents wield weapons designed to kill in war. Morality, I suggest, or at least the power of our urge constantly to moralise, may largely be driven by McDonald emotions. Rather than a mark of humans' transcendence of our animal origins, it may well be, in some regards, a noxious vestige of what was once adaptive. That is not to deny that for our social species to thrive, it must have acquired dispositions that make social life possible.

Let us therefore return to some of the items in our emotional repertoire, and ask how likely they are to serve our purposes in human life as it exists now, when most aspects of life are vastly different from what they were in the environment of evolutionary adaptation.

MORALITY AS A VESTIGE OF BIO-SOCIAL EVOLUTION

Animals living in groups inevitably affect one another's welfare, and so will benefit from a widely distributed capacity to care about one another's needs. Empathy, minimally understood as a sensitivity to others' distress, would foster such a capacity. As we saw in Chapter 6, even rats will sacrifice a treat to avoid subjecting another individual to a painful shock (Hernandez-Lallement et al., 2020). Many other animals share a recognisable form of the emotional disposition to avoid causing harm. That disposition is at the core of the first of five domains of morality which, as we saw in Chapter 4, have been identified by social science (Haidt & Joseph 2007).

What of the other four? A *concern for fairness*, distinct from mere envy, is certainly present in most human subjects. It induces individuals to reject an unfair proposal even when the unfairness favours themselves. In that full sense, it has not clearly been shown to exist in other species (Brosnan, 2006). But chimps are part of the way there, in that they respond far more intensely to being deprived of a reward when they see others getting it. A true sense of fairness may well require inferences to abstract generalisations—*if I don't want to be treated unfairly, and you are not relevantly different, then I don't want you to be treated unfairly*. Such logical moves might be difficult or impossible without language.

So-called alpha individuals exert a form of domination that does not rely on brute force. In groups of apes and other social animals, a homologue of *authority* or *hierarchy* is clearly driven by strong emotions that regulate interactions between members of a tribe.

Loyalty is also clearly sustained in other species by emotions that reinforce solidarity among a group or tribe. As in humans, it is all too compatible with murderous hostility to outsiders.

The case of *purity* is less clear. Disgust is first a response to noxious stimuli. In humans, disgust at moral impurity is triggered not by physical substances but by violations of the sacred, and particularly when those violations involve sex. Both the sacred and sexuality evoke powerfully ambivalent responses. These are often manifested in language. Curse words are frequently drawn from both sex and the sacred. Both the English word 'swear' and the French 'jurer' can mean either 'take an oath' or 'utter a curse word'. Older English curse words often derived from references to the divine ('bloody', 'zounds', 'jeez'), while modern ones are more likely to borrowed from the language of sex.

The embroilment of sex and the sacred is difficult to explain. What is clear from the daily news is that when religious beliefs are linked to emotional attitudes toward sex, they motivate the most violent responses. There is little consensus about the origins of the emotions involved in the concern with moral purity (Ryan & Jethá, 2010; Graeber & Wengrow, 2021). But whatever the biological origins may be of that domain of morality, it seems remarkably inaccessible to rational justification. Human obsessions with purity and the sacred may be unique to humans, but that doesn't make them anything a moralist should be boasting about.

In sum, with one exception, the emotional dispositions that motivate most moral responses are present in at least embryonic form in non-human species. The one exception, purity, remains in need of explanation. But its noxious effects don't provide much reason to extol it as instantiating the higher gift of Human Reason. The biological origins of our penchant for moral judgment does not mark it as worth preserving. It may be a McDonald trait: though once selected for, it no longer serves any purpose and may now be harmful. Indeed, given the greater sophistication of our capacity to inflict harm, the moral emotions that once sustained social life have now become more likely to undermine it. If so, perhaps we should regard our fondness for moralising as one best set aside.

REACTIVE ATTITUDES AND THE USES OF BLAME

But surely, you may protest, some acts *deserve* blame and punishment! Despite our inability clearly to demarcate moral wrongs from other failures, we judge others, and even ourselves, as apt to deserve praise or blame. We allow that an agent's responsibility can have been impaired by some measure of ignorance or compulsion. We no longer regard a starving person who stole a loaf of bread as deserving death or hard labour. Yet most of us, unless we have opted for amoralism, believe that blaming has its uses. We take it for granted that human agents have 'free will', if only to the extent that guilt and shame can shape future behaviour. Blame is an effective tool of manipulation. Other purposeful expressions of emotion, providing they are convincing if not necessarily sincere, can often work too. Even if free will is an illusion, and the social role of emotional expression never rises above the level of more or less intentional manipulation, blame, guilt and shame remain effective means of control.

A more encouraging line of thought, traceable to a famous lecture by Peter Strawson (1919–2006), proposes that 'reactive attitudes', such as blame, resentment and anger, function as a kind of social glue that cannot be dispensed with (Strawson, 1962). Even if no one really can help doing what they do, the perdurance of social cohesion requires that we pretend otherwise and respond accordingly. Some, indeed, have argued that a wrongdoer deserves blame as a mark of respect. Blame, on this view, confirms the wrongdoer's status as a responsible and autonomous member of the community. It honours the agent by treating them as if they were capable of acting rightly (Houston, 1992). Since insects or inanimate objects that have caused harm are not owed that form of respect, withholding blame could be a sign of contempt, not compassion.

It is also, incidentally, what a court of law is expected to do in those cases where an offender is deemed to have been insane. Not that judges (or anyone else) are very good at getting those cases right. Consider Andrea Yates, condemned to life imprisonment in Texas in 2002 for having drowned her five children in the bathtub. Yates had heard voices that commanded her to drown her children in order to save them from Satan. Her insanity defence was initially rejected, because she had executed her project with methodical deliberation (drowning the eldest first), proving that she was fully aware of what she was doing. The jury reasoned that she could not have been insane, since she had acted *rationally* in the light of her goal. But was it not her project itself that was insane? Can we not hope to define objective standards of sanity, as well as of morality? Could we not limit moral blame to actions of sane rational agents endowed at least limited powers of choice based on a grasp of reality?

The answer is not obvious. Andrea Yates was unlucky in that the psychosis from which she suffered was idiosyncratic. Too bad for her that it was not part of a collective delusion. What passes for sanity, like what passes for morality, depends on local culture. Neither Agamemnon nor Abraham has been judged to have been insane or criminal, despite their intention (thwarted in the latter but achieved by the former) of killing their child on a word from the divine. When enough people share a psychotic delusion, they just get a 'religious' tax exemption. Morality, the ghost of religion, seems to define similarly shifting standards of sanity and responsibility. (And can't even get you a tax break.)

As a practical tool designed to influence behaviour, then, blame can serve a useful purpose by eliciting so-called moral emotions such as guilt. Insofar as it simply exploits habits of expectation in social intercourse, the use of blame is entirely compatible with a fictionalist or abolitionist perspective on morality. Neither guilt nor shame, in any case, any more than anger and resentment, is necessarily tied to the moral domain. It is perfectly possible to shame someone for their appearance, their ethnicity, their sexual orientation, gender identity, or any of a host of other characteristics over which the person shamed can exert no control. But as an amoralist, you will recognise these manoeuvres for what they are: tools of manipulation. It is up to you to decide whether using them is something that you really want.

AMORALITY IS NOT INDIFFERENCE

Abjuring the right to blame does not mean you can't take sides. While an amoralist will refrain from claiming that some practice is immoral, they may still, without incoherence, fight with passionate conviction to outlaw it. For example,

an amoralist might advocate legislation to stop genital muti-
lation, or the banning of books, or the persecution of trans
persons. To reject morality is not to reject the power of reasons, of which life provides a ceaseless flow. These include,
for the amoralist no less than for the moralist, reasons that
you already have, including reasons to care about the welfare
of others as well as your own, and to respond to their plight
with compassion, understanding and sometimes rage. For as
I stressed in Chapter 6, those are grounded in the very natural
facts on which moral reasons are supposed to supervene. And
sometimes, you may want to modify the weight you assign to
some of your reasons.

THE CONSEQUENCES OF PRAISE OR BLAME

If you do decide to use the psychological tools of praise or blame,
you may also want to make sure you can tell when an agent has
acted freely—however that difficult notion might be meaningfully construed. There are other features of our psychological
dispositions to cast blame that make it problematic even if we
take an entirely transactional or fictionalist view of their function. These take the form of cases where praise and blame fail
of their instrumental goal. Consider just two examples.

One very straightforward problem arises from a well-
known statistical illusion. It can occur when we observe how
praise and blame affect the learning of a skill. This can be
nicely illustrated by the case of the Naive Flying Instructors
(NFIs). They had noticed that praise for a particularly smooth
landing tends to be followed by one less smooth, while blame
for particularly poor performance is generally followed
by improvement.

The NFIs were understandably tempted to conclude
that blame works to improve performance, but praise only

undermines it. Any student of statistics, however, will point out that the NFIs' observations show nothing of the kind. For what they have observed is exactly what is to be expected of logic and pure chance. By definition, the *worst* performance must be followed by a better one, and the *best* can only be followed by one less good. That is one aspect of the statistical truism that goes by the name of 'regression to the mean': in any random distribution, there are more things in the middle than at the edges of the bell curve (Kahneman, 2011, p. 175).

A second and more intriguing psychological quirk in our disposition to praise or blame is known as the Knobe effect, after the philosopher Joshua Knobe who discovered it. While I have expressed some doubts about our ability to ascribe genuine responsibility based on an attribution of free will, I have so far taken it for granted that an agent is appropriately held responsible only for an intentional action. (Setting aside refinements that might require us to distinguish negligence, inadvertence, distraction, etc. as creating degrees of intentionality.) What Knobe showed is that this connection is sometimes reversed: we are more likely to believe that an agent did something intentionally when we believe the act was morally wrong. An especially intriguing illustration is provided by an experiment in which one group of subjects were presented with the following vignette:

> The vice-president of a company went to the chairman of the board and said, 'We are thinking of starting a new program. It will help us increase profits, but it will also harm the environment.' The chairman of the board answered, 'I don't care at all about harming the environment. I just want to make as much profit as I can. Let's

start the new program.' They started the new program. Sure enough, the environment was harmed.

(Knobe, 2003, p. 191)

Subjects in a second group were offered the very same vignette, except for the substitution of the word 'help' for 'harm'. Subjects were then asked how much praise or blame the chairman deserved for proceeding with the program in the 'harm' condition, and also whether the harm had been intentional. Over 80 per cent of subjects interviewed opted to blame the chairman and judged the decision to have been intentional. In the 'help' condition, almost as many (77%) came to the opposite conclusion: they deemed the decision's helpful outcome to have been unintentional and deserving of no praise.

It seems, then, that there is a radical asymmetry between cases where a predictable side effect is judged morally wrong and those where it is regarded as potentially praiseworthy. Observers judge a side effect to have been more intentional, and thus more worthy of blame, if they judge it to be morally wrong. If they deem it to be morally good, the corresponding praise for something done intentionally is less likely to be forthcoming. While an act has to be intentional in order to be praised or blamed, it will be less likely to be judged intentional if the effect is deemed praiseworthy, and more likely to be judged intentional if the side effect is deemed blameable (Knobe, 2003; Pettit & Knobe, 2009).

This asymmetry obviously undermines the average observer's ability to assign praise or blame in a consistent and rational way. It may have occurred to you that if you are an amoralist, you have refrained from moral appraisal altogether. You are thus safe from the Knobe effect.

It remains to be seen, of course, whether professing amoralism is sufficient to protect one from the Knobe effect. Even the most sincere Abelief, as we have seen in previous chapters, is but an unreliable attempt to regiment explicitly the true state of an agent's Pbelief. Given the deep evolutionary origins of the emotions that power morality, you may not find it easy to do away with guilt, resentment or the lust for revenge and punishment of transgressions you were brought up to deem immoral.

If we are to believe the wisdom of great minds as far away from one another as Aeschylus and Nietzsche, the legal institutions set up to promote justice, and particularly retributive punishment, are best understood as ways of civilising those dark moral passions and making them less destructive. Atavistic emotions are not easily cast off. The best we can hope for may be to become aware of their regrettable features. You can at least cease to regard yourself as morally entitled to cast blame all around you whenever something displeases you and you've got Morality to back you up.

You can at least, in other words, try to curb your moralistic attitudes. If you succeed in doing so, and manage to resist the temptation to paint everything in the world as moral or immoral, you may gradually acquire the ability to live as an amoralist. Should you undertake to try, I conclude with a few pieces of advice. They can be read as the then . . . clauses of conditionals of which the antecedent reads: If you want to be amoral, then . . .

HOW TO BE AMORAL: SOME PRACTICAL SUGGESTIONS

- Start by acknowledging the non-existence of moral facts. There are practical conditionals that can clarify and refine your reasons to act, but there are no moral imperatives, no commands in the absence of commanders.

- Do not give up on deciding what you want, and how rational you want your wants to be.
- Own your reasons. Let them be *your* reasons. Since there is no moral domain to demarcate, forget worrying about the moral status of your reasons.
- If you criticise others, focus only on their internal reasons. Do not presume to tell them what those should have been. They can be convicted of irrationality only in terms of their own reasons, when they are brought to make inconsistent claims about their own beliefs and wants.
- Don't take your explicit reasons, or those avowed by others, to be the last word on the real reasons that govern what you or others do.
- Retire, as much as possible, words the use of which is tainted with moral disapproval. Some examples:

  o Substitute *want* for *ought*, *should* or *must*, except in those contexts where the latter are clearly to be taken as merely expressing factual expectation or instrumental conditions.

  o Substitute *regret* for *guilt*. The word *shame* is trickier, because even moralists agree that shame typically pertains to who you are, over which you may have no control, rather than what you did, for which you are presumed responsible. So you might want to renounce *shame* and shaming even if you don't discard morality.

  o For talk of *rights*, substitute an invitation to empathise with what others may want. This one may be hardest to give up. For talk of rights often just expresses a desperate plea against callous indifference.

- **This Above All:**
  - o Renounce the attitude of entitlement that comes from the conviction that your principles derive from an objective moral reality, capable of giving your life meaning. There is no Moral Truth to lend your judgment authority or outweigh 'mere' wants.
  - o There are only wants all the way down. (Or up.) That is not to deny that your wants emerge out of the huge ocean of native inclinations and social influences into which you were plunged in kindergarten, and before, and ever since.
  - o To overcome your moralising instinct, go 'meta' or second order: if you must indulge it, use it to quell your urge to moralise itself.

Notes

1

1. For recent work on moral realism among common folks, see Pölzler and Wright (2020).
2. For a book-length defence of the primacy of reasons over values or moral oughts, sometimes referred to as 'buck-passing', see Rowland (2018).
3. The two ways of understanding 'The King of France is bald'—as false, or as neither true nor false, go back to Bertrand Russell and Peter Strawson respectively. (See Russell, 1905; Strawson, 1950, and Russell's 1957 witty if uncomprehending riposte.)
4. For any sticklers who might pounce with the *gotcha* that 'God does not exist' cannot then be true either, logicians have an answer: an existence statement is not really about a thing but a concept. 'X does not exist' can be adequately glossed as asserting that 'the concept of X is empty' or 'the expression "X" lacks a referent'. It is also notable that some theologians, while believing that God exists, deny that anything (else) can be truly said about him. That view is known as 'Apophatism'.
5. 'Surprising as it may seem, countries that are less religious actually tend to be less corrupt and have lower murder rates than religious ones' (Inglehart, 2020, p. 111).
6. For what it's worth, according to a series of empirical investigations, moral philosophers do no better than other professors. A study concludes: 'It remains to be shown that even a lifetime's worth of philosophical moral reflection has any influence upon one's real world moral behavior' (Schwitzgebel & Rust, 2014, p. 320).

2

1. www.renemagritte.org/the-castle-of-the-pyrenees.jsp#prettyPhoto [image1]/0.

2. For an online summary, see www.bethinking.org/bible/old-testament-mass-killings.

3. Stoicism, a school of philosophy perhaps even more influential in Ancient Greece and Rome than the Platonic or the Aristotelian, also emphasises the importance of 'Living according to nature'. It has undergone a modern revival (Gill, 2022). But Stoicism takes the idea in very different directions from either Natural Law or Evolutionary Ethics. As it is far less representative of the sort of moral systems that are my targets here, I do not discuss it. But see the section on 'Ethics' in *Durand, Shogry and Baltzly (2023).

4. The classic exposition of this view, named 'aetiological' because it explains functions and goal-directed processes in causal terms that require no magic influence of future ends or goals, is that of Ruth Millikan (Millikan, 1984). See also *Allen and Neal (2020).

5. On the importance of the ESS that balances exploration and imitation, see Boyd and Richerson (2005).

6. For a contrary argument, defending a version of evolutionary ethics, see Thompson (2022). On ways in which evolution might be relevant to ethics, see *Alexander (2020).

7. The other definition I remember from my childhood is that you could tell a gentleman by his shoes. Presumably because a gentleman would have a butler to shine them.

8. For a comprehensive introduction to Contractarianism, see *Cudd and Eftekhari (2021).

3

1. Or perhaps not. But to deny this is paradoxical enough to be amusing, as in the case of the great physicist Niels Bohr, who was reputed to have sported a lucky horseshoe on his front door. When challenged about his superstition, he would reply, 'Of course I don't believe it. But apparently it works even if you don't believe it.'

2. Although long taken for granted, this is now being questioned in some quarters (Andrews, 2023).

3. This is the way that George Berkeley (1685–1753), who held that *to be is to be perceived*, resolved the question of how anything could exist unperceived. It was nicely captured by a pair of limericks by the theologian Ronald Knox (1888–1957): 'There was a young man who said "God / Must find it exceedingly odd / To think that the tree / Should continue to be / When there's no one about in the quad." Reply: "Dear Sir: Your astonishment's odd; / I am always about in the quad. / And that's why the tree / Will continue to be / Since observed by, Yours faithfully, God."'

4. On the objective status of facts created by social institutions, see Searle (2010).

4

1. See www.treehugger.com/sustainable-vanilla-5217517; www.smith sonianmag.com/science-nature/bittersweet-story-vanilla-180962757; www.iucn.org/news/species/202007/almost-a-third-lemurs-and-north-atlantic-right-whale-now-critically-endangered-iucn-red-list.

2. https://foodispower.org/human-labor-slavery/slavery-chocolate.

3. I refrain here from engaging with further problems raised by the formula's limitation to human lives. Many influential utilitarians, including Mill himself and his predecessor Jeremy Bentham (1748–1832), hold that other sentient beings should be included in the calculus.

4. For a sketch of the butterfly effect and its significance, see https:// fs.blog/the-butterfly-effect/#:~:text=It%20is%20a%20tenet%20of, cause%20a%20tornado%20in%20Texas.

5. See Wilkerson (2020), especially chapter 15, for particularly brutal examples.

6. See www.thelifeyoucansave.org/take-the-pledge.

5

1. Bayesian Decision Theory is so called because it is part of a broader theory that makes crucial use of a theorem by Thomas Bayes (1701–1761) relating the probability of a hypothesis on evidence [Prob(H/E)] to its converse, the likelihood of that evidence if the hypothesis is true [Prob(E/H)]. See *Steele and Stefánsson (2020) and Box #3 in Chapter 4.

2. I am here ignoring a complication. While 'degree of belief' usually refers to subjective probability as discussed in Frank P. Ramsey's paper 'Truth and Probability' (Ramsey, 1990), another dimension of degree of belief was introduced by Isaac Levi (1930–2018), referring to the *confidence* or stability of a given probability assignment (Levi, 1967). Your bet on Tails might reflect the same 0.5 probability when flipping an unseen coin as for one that you have already thrown a thousand times (getting, say, 470 Tails to 530 Heads). But if you then get an unlikely straight run of Heads in the next ten throws, of which the statistical probability is 1/1024, that might change your assessment of probability in the first case (perhaps the coin is biased), but it will leave it unchanged in the second (when the coin's fairness has been tested). I ignore this, because it affects only the stability of a Pbelief, not its value at given moment.

6

1. 'Rationalisation' is here used as a thick concept, implying a discrepancy between the justifying reason offered and the causally effective motivation that led to action. In the last chapter, it was used without the same pejorative connotation, to refer to what may be our best sincere effort at verbalising one's effective reasons.

7

1. A notable exception is Nietzsche: 'It has gradually become clear to me what every great philosophy has hitherto been: a confession on the part of its author and a kind of involuntary and unconscious memoir' (Nietzsche 2003 [1886], §6).

References

Alexander, J. M. (2020). Evolutionary Game Theory. In E. N. Zalta (ed.), *The Stanford Encyclopedia of Philosophy* (Summer 2021 Edition). https://plato.stanford.edu/archives/sum2021/entries/game-evolutionary

Allen, C., & Neal, J. (2020). Teleological Notions in Biology. In E. N. Zalta (ed.), *The Stanford Encyclopedia of Philosophy* (Spring 2020 Edition). https://plato.stanford.edu/archives/spr2020/entries/teleology-biology

Andrews, K. (2020). Naive normativity: The social foundations of moral cognition. *Journal of the American Philosophical Association*, 6(1), 36–56. https://doi.org/10.1017/apa.2019.30

Andrews, K. (2023). What is it like to be a crab? AEON, 20 November. Retrieved from https://aeon.co/essays/are-we-ready-to-study-consciousness-in-crabs-and-the-like

Aristotle. (1984). Metaphysics. In J. Barnes (ed.), *The Complete Works of Aristotle: The Revised Oxford Translation*. Bollingen Series. Princeton: Princeton University Press.

Ayala, F. (2010) The Difference of Being Human: Morality. *Proceedings of the National Academy of Sciences*, 107 (Supplement 2), 9015–22.

Ayer, A. J. (1936). *Language, Truth and Logic*. London: Gollancz.

Benatar, D. (2006). *Better Never to Have Been*. Oxford: Oxford University Press.

Bennett, J. (1974). The conscience of Huckleberry Finn. *Philosophy*, 49, 123–34.

Boyd, R., & Richerson, P. J. (2005). Rationality, Imitation and Tradition. In *The Origin and Evolution of Cultures* (pp. 379–96). Oxford; New York: Oxford University Press.

Brosnan, S. F. (2006). Nonhuman species' reactions to inequity and their implications for fairness. *Social Justice Research*, 19(2), 153–85.

Butler, S. (1872). *Erewhon*. London: Trübner.

Chang, R. (2004). Can desires provide reasons for actions. In R. J. Wallace, P. Pettit, S. Scheffler & M. Smith (eds), *Reason and Value: Themes from the Philosophy of Joseph Raz* (pp. 56–90). Oxford: Clarendon Press.

Chignell, A. (2018). The Ethics of Belief. In E. N. Zalta (ed.), *The Stanford Encyclopedia of Philosophy* (Spring 2018 Edition). https://plato.stanford.edu/archives/spr2018/entries/ethics-belief

Cudd, A., & Eftekhari, S. (2021). Contractarianism. In E. N. Zalta (ed.), *The Stanford Encyclopedia of Philosophy* (Winter 2021 Edition). https://plato.stanford.edu/archives/win2021/entries/contractarianism

D'Arms, J., & Jacobson, D. (2007). Sensibility theory and projectivism. In D. Copp (ed.), *The Oxford Handbook of Ethical Theory* (pp. 186–218). New York: Oxford University Press. http://dx.doi.org/10.1093/oxfordhb/9780195325911.003.0008

Dennett, D. C. (2006). *Breaking the Spell: Religion as a Natural Phenomenon.* New York: Viking.

Dissanayake, E. (2000). *Art and Intimacy: How the Arts Began.* Seattle; London: University of Washington Press.

Durand, M., Shogry, S., & Baltzly, D. (2023). Stoicism. In E. N. Zalta (ed.), *The Stanford Encyclopedia of Philosophy* (Spring 2023 Edition). https://plato.stanford.edu/archives/sr2023/entries/stoicism

Edmonds, D. (2023). *Parfit: A Philosopher and His Mission to Save Morality.* Princeton, NJ: Princeton University Press.

Evans, J. S. B. T. (2018). Dual Process theory: Perspectives and problems. In W. DeNeys (ed.), *Dual Process Theory 2.0* (pp. 137–56). London: Routledge.

Finlay, S., & Schroeder, M. (2017). Reasons for Action: Internal vs. External. In Edward N. Zalta (ed.), *The Stanford Encyclopedia of Philosophy* (Fall 2017 Edition). https://plato.stanford.edu/archives/fall2017/entries/reasons-internal-external

Garner, R., & Joyce, R. (eds). (2019). *The End of Morality: Taking Moral Abolitionism Seriously.* London; New York: Routledge.

Gauthier, D. (1987). *Morals by Agreement.* Oxford: Oxford University Press.

Gert, B. (2005). *Morality: Its Nature and Justification.* New York: Oxford University Press.

Gervais, W. M. (2014). Everything is permitted? People intuitively judge immorality as representative of atheists. *PLOS One, 9*(4), e92302. https://doi.org/10.1371%2Fjournal.pone.0092302

Gill, C. (2022). *Learning to Live Naturally: Stoic Ethics and Its Modern Significance.* New York: Oxford University Press.

Gilligan, C. (1982). *In a Different Voice: Psychological Theory and Women's Development.* Cambridge, MA: Harvard University Press.

Goldman, A. (2009, October). Desires and reasons. *American Philosophical Quarterly*, 46(4), 291–304.

Gowans, C. (2021). Moral Relativism. In E. N. Zalta (ed.), *The Stanford Encyclopedia of Philosophy (Spring 2021 Edition)*. https://plato.stanford.edu/archives/spr2021/entries/moral-relativism

Graeber, D., & Wengrow, D. (2021). *The Dawn of Everything: A New History of Humanity.* New York: Farrar Straus and Giroux.

Grandin, T., & Johnson, C. (2005). *Animals in Translation: Using the Mysteries of Autism to Decode Animal Behavior.* New York: Scribner.

Haidt, J., & Björklund, F. (2008). Social Intuitionists Answer Six Questions about Moral Psychology. In W. Sinnott-Armstrong (ed.), *Moral Psychology, Vol. 2* (pp. 181–217). Cambridge, MA: MIT Press.

Haidt, J., & Joseph, C. (2007). The moral mind: How five sets of innate intuitions guide the development of many culture-specific virtues, and perhaps even modules. In P. Carruthers, S. Laurence & S. Stich (eds), *The Innate Mind: Foundations and the Future, Vol. 3* (pp. 367–92). Oxford; New York: Oxford University Press.

Hare, R. D., and Babiak, P. (2006). *Snakes in Suits.* New York: Harper Collins.

Hare, R. M. (1952). *The Language of Morals.* Oxford: Clarendon Press.

Henrich, J. (2020). *The WEIRDest people in the world: How the West Became Psychologically Peculiar and Particularly Prosperous.* New York: Farrar Straus.

Hernandez-Lallement, J., Attah, A., Soyman, E., Pinhal, C., Gazzola, V., & Keysers, C. (2020). Harm to others acts as a negative reinforcer in rats. *Current Biology*, 30(6), 949–61.E7. https://doi.org/10.1016/j.cub.2020.01.017

Hirstein, W. (2005). *Brain Fiction: Self-Deception and the Riddle of Confabulation.* Cambridge, MA: MIT Press.

Hooker, B. (2023). Rule Consequentialism. In E. N. Zalta (ed.), *The Stanford Encyclopedia of Philosophy (Spring 2023 Edition)*. https://plato.stanford.edu/archives/spr2023/entries/consequentialism-rule

Houston, B. (1992). In praise of blame. *Hypatia*, 7(2), 128–47.

Hume, D. (1978 [1739]). *A Treatise of Human Nature*, ed. L. A. Selby-Bigge, revised by & notes by P. H. Nidditch. (2nd ed.). Oxford: Oxford University Press.

Hursthouse, R., & Pettigrove, G. (2018). Virtue Ethics. In E. N. Zalta (ed.), *The Stanford Encyclopedia of Philosophy (Winter 2018 Edition)*. https://plato.stanford.edu/archives/win2018/entries/ethics-virtue

Ichikawa, J. J., & Steup, M. (2018). The Analysis of Knowledge. In E. N. Zalta (Ed.), *The Stanford Encyclopedia of Philosophy* (Summer 2018 Edition). https://plato.stanford.edu/archives/sum2018/entries/knowledge-analysis

Inglehart, R. F. (2020). Giving Up on God: The Global Decline of Religion. *Foreign Affairs*, 99(5), 110–18.

Jacob, F. (1976). *The Logic of Life: A History of Heredity*, trans. B. E. Spillman. New York: Vintage.

John Paul II, Pope. (1984). *Salvifici doloris* [Apostolic Letter]. Vatican: Holy See.

Joyce, R. (2006). *The Evolution of Morality*. Cambridge, MA: MIT Press.

Joyce, R. (2019). Moral fictionalism: How to have your cake and eat it too. In R. Garner & R. Joyce (eds), *The End of Morality: Taking Moral Abolitionism Seriously* (pp. 150–65). New York; London: Routledge.

Kahneman, D. (2011). *Thinking, Fast and Slow*. New York; Toronto: Farrar, Straus and Giroux.

Kant, I. (1998 [1785]). *The Metaphysics of Morals*, trans. Mary J. Gregor, introduction by Roger J. Sullivan. Cambridge: Cambridge University Press.

Kment, B. (2021). Varieties of Modality. In E. N. Zalta (Ed.). *The Stanford Encyclopedia of Philosophy* (Spring 2021 Edition). https://Plato.Stanford.Edu/Archives/Spr2021/Entries/Modality-Varieties

Knobe, J. (2003). Intentional action in folk psychology: An experimental investigation. *Philosophical Psychology*, 16, 309–23.

Kraut, R. (2012). *Against Absolute Goodness*. New York: Oxford University Press. https://doi.org/10.1093/acprof:oso/9780199844463.001.0001

Levi, I. (1967). *Gambling with Truth: An Essay on Induction and the Aims of Science*. New York: Knopf.

MacAskill, W. (2022). The case for long-termism. *The New York Times*, 8 May. www.nytimes.com/2022/08/05/opinion/the-case-for-long termism.html

Mackie, J. L. (1977). *Ethics: Inventing Right and Wrong*. Harmondsworth: Penguin.

Marks, J. (2012). *Ethics Without Morals*. London; New York: Routledge.

Marks, J. (2016). *Hard Atheism and the Ethics of Desire: An Alternative to Morality*. Cham, Switzerland: Palgrave Macmillan.

Matthen, M. (2024). The emergence of tastes. In *The Geography of Taste*, ed. D. L. McIver, S. Matherne, M. Matthen, B. Nanay, Bence. New York: Oxford University Press, pp. 27–55.

Maynard Smith, J. (1984). Game theory and the evolution of behavior. *The Behavioral and Brain Sciences*, 7, 95–126.

Why It's OK to Be Amoral

McPherson, T. (2019). Supervenience in Ethics. In E. N. Zalta (ed.), *The Stanford Encyclopedia of Philosophy (Winter 2019 Edition)*. https://plato. stanford.edu/archives/win2019/entries/supervenience-ethics

Mill, J. S. (1991 [1861]). *Collected Works of John Stuart Mill: Vol. 10. Utilitarianism*, ed. J. Robson. University of Toronto Press.

Miller, G. A. (1956). The magical number seven, plus or minus two: Some limits on our capacity for processing information. *Psychological Review*, 63, 81–97.

Millikan, R. G. (1984). *Language, Thought, and Other Biological Categories*. Cambridge, MA: MIT Press, A Bradford Book.

Nietzsche, F. (1998 [1887]). *On the Genealogy of Morality*, trans. and notes by M. Clark & A. J. Swensen. Indianapolis, IN: Hackett.

Nietzsche, F. (2003 [1886]). *Beyond Good and Evil: Prelude to a Philosophy of the Future*, trans. R. J. Hollingdale. London; New York: Penguin Books.

Nisbett, R. E., & Wilson, T. D. (1977). Telling more than we can know: Verbal reports on mental states. *Psychological Review*, 84(3), 231–59.

Noddings, N. (1983). *Caring: A Feminine Approach to Ethics and Moral Education*. Berkeley: University of California Press.

Norlock, K. (2019). Feminist Ethics. In E. N. Zalta (ed.), *The Stanford Encyclopedia of Philosophy (Summer 1919 Edition)*. https://plato.stanford.edu/ archives/sum2019/entries/feminism-ethics

Nussbaum, M. C. (1978). *Aristotle's De Motu Animalium: Text with translation, commentary, and interpretive essays*. Princeton, NJ: Princeton University Press.

Oberheim, E., & Hoyningen-Huene, P. (2018). The Incommensurability of Scientific Theories. In E. N. Zalta (ed.), *The Stanford Encyclopedia of Philosophy (Fall 2018 Edition)*. https://plato.stanford.edu/archives/fall 2018/entries/incommensurability

Pettit, D., & Knobe, J. (2009). The pervasive impact of moral judgment. *Mind and Language*, 24(5), 586–604.

Pinker, S. (2008). The moral instinct. *The New York Times Magazine*, 1 January. www.nytimes.com/2008/01/13/magazine/13Psychology-t.html

Plato. (1997a). *Euthyphro* (G. Grube, trans.). In *Complete Works*, ed. J. M. Cooper & D. Hutchinson (pp. 1–16). Indianapolis, IN: Hackett.

Plato. (1997b). *Meno* (G. Grube, trans.). In *Complete Works*, ed. J. M. Cooper & D. Hutchinson (pp. 870–896). Indianapolis, IN: Hackett.

Pölzler, T., & Wright, J. C. (2020). Anti-Realist Pluralism: A New Approach to Folk Metaethics. *Review of Philosophy and Psychology*, 11(1), 53–82. https://doi.org/10.1007/s13164-019-00447-8

Ramsey, F. P. (1990). Truth and probability. In H. Mellor (ed.), *Philosophical Papers* (pp. 52–93). Cambridge: Cambridge University Press.

Rawls, J. (1977). *A Theory of Justice*. Cambridge, MA: Harvard University Press.

Rowland, R. (2018). *The Normative and the Evaluative: The Buck-Passing Account of Value*. Oxford: Oxford University Press.

Russell, B. (1905). On denoting. Mind, 14(56), 479–93.

Russell, B. (1957). Mr. Strawson on referring. Mind, 67(263), 385–9.

Ryan, C., & Jethá, C. (2010). *Sex at Dawn: The Prehistoric Origins of modern sexuality*. New York: Harper.

Schroeder, M. (2021). Value Theory. In E. N. Zalta (ed.), *The Stanford Encyclopedia of Philosophy (Fall 2021 Edition)*. https://plato.stanford.edu/archives/fall2021/entries/value-theory

Schwitzgebel, E., & Rust, J. (2014). The moral behavior of ethics professors: Relationships among self-reported behavior, expressed normative attitude, and directly observed behavior. *Philosophical Psychology*, 27(3), 293–327. https://doi.org/10.1080/09515089.2012.727135

Searle, J. R. (2010). *Making the Social World*. Oxford: Oxford University Press.

Shweder, R. A., Much, N. C., Mahapatra, M., & Park, L. (2000). The 'Big Three' of morality (autonomy, community, divinity) and the 'Big Three' explanations of suffering. In R. A. Shweder, *Why Do Men Barbecue? Recipes for Cultural Psychology* (pp. 120–69). New York: Routledge.

Singer, P. (2009). The life you can save. *The New York Times*, 10 March. www.nytimes.com/2009/03/11/books/chapters/chapter-life-you-could-save.html

Spinoza, B. de. (2020). Treatise on the emendation of the intellect. In E. Curley (ed.), *A Spinoza Reader: The Ethics and Other Works*. Princeton, NJ: Princeton University Press.

Steele, K., & Stefánsson, H. O. (2020). Decision Theory. In E. N. Zalta (Ed.), *The Stanford Encyclopedia of Philosophy (Winter 2020 Edition)*. https://plato.stanford.edu/archives/win2020/entries/decision-theory

Stevenson, C. (1944). *Ethics and Language*. New Haven, CT: Yale University Press.

Strawson, P. F. (1950). On Referring. In *Essays in Conceptual Analysis*, ed. A.P. Martinich and Anthony Flew (2nd ed.). London: Macmillan.

Strawson, P. F. (1962). *Freedom and Resentment*. Annual philosophical lecture, Henriette Hertz trust 1962. London: Oxford University Press.

Styron, W. (1980). *Sophie's Choice*. New York: Bantam.

Thompson, R. P. (2022). *Evolution, Morality and the Fabric of Society*. Cambridge: Cambridge University Press.

Torres, É. P. (2022, 20/11). What the Sam Bankman-Fried debacle can teach us about 'longtermism'. *Salon*. www.salon.com/2022/11/20/what-the-sam-bankman-fried-debacle-can-teach-us-about-longtermism

Turiel, E. (1983). *The Development of Social Knowledge: Morality and Convention*. Cambridge: Cambridge University Press.

van Fraassen, B. C. (1984). Belief and the Will. *Journal of Philosophy*, 81(5), 235–56.

Väyrynen, P. (2021). Thick Ethical Concepts. In *The Stanford Encyclopedia of Philosophy (Spring 2021 Edition)*. https://plato.stanford.edu/archives/spr2021/entries/thick-ethical-concepts

Wilkerson, I. (2020). *Caste: The Origins of Our Discontents*. New York: Random House.

Wolf, S. (2015). Moral Saints. In *The Variety of Values: Essays on Morality, Meaning, and Love* (pp. 11–30). New York: Oxford University Press.

Yu, A. (2007). Adaptive behavior: Humans act as Bayesian learners. *Current Biology*, 17, 977–80.

Ziff, P. (1960). *Semantic Analysis*. Ithaca, NY: Cornell University Press.

Index

Printed in the United States
by Baker & Taylor Publisher Services